New Creature

All Things Become New

Matthew Whitaker

Copyright © 2018 by Matthew Whitaker
All rights reserved

Rejoice Essential Publishing
P.O. BOX 512
Effingham, SC 29541
www.republishing.org

All rights reserved. No part of this book may be used or reproduced by any means, graphic, electronic, or mechanical, including photocopying, recording, taping or by any information storage retrieval system without the written permission of the publisher except in the case of brief quotations embodied in critical articles and reviews.

Scripture quotations marked (NIV) are taken from the Holy Bible, New International Version®, NIV®. Copyright ©1973, 1978, 1984, 2011 by Biblica, Inc.™ Used by permission of Zondervan. All rights reserved.

Scripture quotations marked (NKJV) are taken from the New King James Version®. Copyright ©1982 by Thomas Nelson. Used by permission. All rights reserved

Author Photo by Candy Dugas/Candy's Photography.

If this book had a positive impact in your life, email author at mjwhit29@gmail.com

Unless otherwise indicated, Scripture is taken from the King James Version

New Creature/ Matthew Whitaker
ISBN-10: 1-946756-52-0
ISBN-13: 978-1-946756-52-7

Library of Congress Control Number: 2019940546

How God Moved Me from Multiple Bondages to Absolute Freedom And You Too Can!— Matt Whitaker

ACKNOWLEDGMENTS

I would like to thank Abba Father for rescuing me out of the mouth of hell, giving me new life, and restoring me back to Your original blueprint. I can hardly imagine where I'd be today without you, Lord. Thank you for saving me, with all my strength, heart and soul I love you my King, my Master, and my Everything; you are beautiful God.

Contents

ACKNOWLEDGMENTS..vii

INTRODUCTION..1

CHAPTER 1: Paint Marks of a Misunderstood Childhood..................................7

CHAPTER 2: Destructive Adolescence..............................10

CHAPTER 3: Where do I belong in life..17

CHAPTER 4: Meandering Further into the World.........................21

CHAPTER 5: Glimmers of Light in Utter Darkness....................27

CHAPTER 6: Rescued out of the Mouth of Hell....................33

CHAPTER 7: A Step of Faith...Faith in Action.................................45

CHAPTER 8:	My Dysfunction Became My Wilderness..................60
CHAPTER 9:	Restoring the Broken Fellowship with Our Creator..................70
CHAPTER 10:	Inner Healing; Uncovering the Wounds..................73
CHAPTER 11:	Unforgiveness..................77
CHAPTER 12:	Purging the Soul..................80
CHAPTER 13:	Fear..................90
CHAPTER 14:	Rejection and Fear Go Hand in Hand..................96
CHAPTER 15:	Slaying the Dragon: Pressing in to Win..................102
CHAPTER 16:	Guarding the Gates..................112
CHAPTER 17:	Marine Spirits..................116
CHAPTER 18:	Ahab Programming; Arrested Development..................133

ABOUT THE AUTHOR..146

Introduction

It must have been somewhere around 2 a.m. when the Holy Spirit spoke to me to give me the title of this book. I must have had seven ideas written down for the title and had nearly settled on "Identity Crisis." When I woke up in the middle of the night to use the bathroom, my mind seemed so consumed with the naming of the book when the still small voice of the Lord broke through and interrupted my thoughts with "New Creature."

Before this divine interruption took place that night, one idea I had for the name of the book was "The Expression of God's Love." I thought to name it that because in essence, this book is the expression of God's love in the form of healing and deliverance. My intent was to prove to believers and nonbelievers that He is able to do the impossible and forgive their sins even after being turned over to a reprobate mind. Many men and women have secret struggles that they have never been able to find deliverance from because they are too afraid to expose these issues to other people in order to find help.

I struggled so much for so long to find true deliverance that when I found it, I developed a passion for seeking out the lost and the wounded to help them get free. Maybe this is you and the Lord has caused this book to fall into your hands because He wants to express His love to you, and He's set to deliver you from the most stubborn, difficult demonic bondages as you read through the pages. My prayer and belief are that many will be set free as a result of this God-inspired word; as God is the author of my life, He wrote it for you.

Or perhaps you are a parent that is brokenhearted and desperately want to find hope for your child who is as lost as I once was. If that's you, you are probably searching for answers and wisdom on how to get through this, what to do, and how to have the strength or faith to simply release your young adult child to the Lord. How do we truly release our children to God? You have to trust God; and to trust God, you have to know Him with all of your heart. You have to know that nothing is too big for God and that your child is just as likely to come to know the Lord and be saved as you or anyone else in this world.

But the key to your child's salvation could be you releasing them, loving them, and praying in secret believing the word of God that says that whatsoever you ask believing in your heart, it shall be done. Whatever you ask, ask in secret and it shall be done openly. You can't force someone to be saved; they have to be drawn by the Father and you can help make that happen by praying. It is my prayer that not only will you find hope and wisdom, but that you might also find yourself inspired to seek the One who created you in a much deeper intimate way, and find yourself delivered and set free by the time you get to the last pages of this book.

If your children see God working in your life, it could be the biggest impact you'll ever have on them. Perhaps your whole family will get restored as a result of the transformation that manifests in your life so that the scripture will be fulfilled that says, if you believe on the Lord Jesus Christ, you shall be saved and your house. Sometimes we can be so focused on our loved ones when we really need to focus on ourselves. Often people are trying to lead other people in the right direction when they themselves haven't ever submitted their whole heart to the Lord to be on the right path. What I am saying is that many people call themselves saved when they are not.

Salvation comes by two things: believing in your heart that Jesus died and rose from the dead, thereby paying the ransom for your sins; and calling Him your Lord and Savior. To call Him Lord comes with a condition. It's a heart condition that brings a drastic change in your life as you become born again. When you start truly calling Him Lord, that's when He takes control of your life and you find yourself no longer leaning on your own intellect but wholly on the Holy Spirit for every direction in your life. How will people see God working in your life if you are still controlling your life? It's simple, they won't. Let this book serve as an unveiling of God's mysteries in your life. I pray that this book pierces the veil and brings you into the newness of life.

Then there are others who have found themselves in the wilderness. Maybe you are one and you just feel lost, scared and stuck in life. As I am writing, I am reminded of a dream I had when I first started writing this book by the prompting of the Holy Spirit and by faith. In this dream, I was standing outside of my car with a friend whom I never saw his face, but only glimpses of his body and garments as he stood to my right talking with me. At the end of our conversation, he said, "Go now, and I'll meet you on the other side." I jumped into my car and headed down a gravel road. Suddenly, the gravel road turned into a rapid moving river and my car transformed into a raft.

Instantly, I found myself going very fast and in each hand was a cord that I would use to steer this raft around curves. If I pulled the cord on the left, I would go left and if I pulled the right cord, the raft would steer to the right. I found myself learning the operations and maneuvering around the curves easily but had to pay close attention and focus on what I was doing .

The interpretation: A road usually represents your path of life and the river represents the fluid path orchestrated by the Holy Spirit. The friend talking with me at the beginning was Jesus who was giving me instructions that were not revealed in the dream, but only as life unfolded. He was letting me know there were going to be some difficult twists and turns, but as long as I yielded to the flow of His Spirit, I would be fine, and that I could feel safe and encouraged knowing that He would meet me on the other side of the process.

As I began writing this book by faith and with the prompting of the Holy Spirit, I found myself in a wilderness situation where I grew much closer to the Lord as I sought Him day and night. Through this wilderness, I found myself in a process of deliverance that was not easy, but necessary as His purifying moment for my life. As I pressed in, the Lord released keys of wisdom to deliverance and I simply wrote about it as I went through the fiery heat of the wilderness. For those that have found themselves in a dysfunctional or a stuck place in life, I believe the Lord had me to write this book for you so you could see that there is a light at the end of the tunnel. Yes, there is an end to this process you've found yourself in, and it is for a greater purpose than you can see from where you are.

Upon finishing this book, I felt led one day to count the chapters to find that it had eighteen chapters and then picked up a book I left sitting on a bench beside my desk. As my attention was drawn to the book with excitement, I sensed the number eighteen was going to speak to confirm the prophetic context of this book. Eighteen in correlation to this book means: Complete new beginning; or Complete putting off of the old self. My question to the body of believers and nonbelievers is, are you living to be all that God created you to be? Are you living out your purpose or are there still barriers to be destroyed in your life so that your fellowship with the Creator of heaven and earth can be restored? Are you tired of your "stuck place?" I declare unto you, it is your time to go forward! I declare RAPID FORWARD MOVEMENT in Jesus' name.

My prayer is that God will take you by the hand and lead you through the processes of life; lead you to a place of salvation, sanctification, and purification; and restore you back to His original blueprint. I pray that you will find yourself being restored back to "in the cool of the day" experience Adam once had at Eden and restore your fellowship with the Creator that you will walk with Him in the garden of intimacy. Lord, take us by the hand and lead us to our destinies.

For I the Lord thy God will hold thy right hand, saying unto thee, Fear not; I will help thee.—Isaiah 41:13

CHAPTER 1

Paint Marks of a Misunderstood Childhood

I grew up in the typical modern-day setting. My parents divorced when I was three years old. Afterwards, my Mother raised my sister and me while my Dad continued serving away from home in the military, which at that time was overseas. There was no one that stepped in to fill that role in my life, so my masculinity was never affirmed. Later on, in adolescence, I began to experience a lot of depression, shame, feelings of not being accepting, and social awkwardness. I felt very inadequate and unsure of things, but did my best to cope with life. When I was five years old, I said to my Mom, "Life would be easier if I were a girl." She asked me why I felt that way, but at the time, I didn't know why. I never actually wanted to be a girl, but for some reason at that age, I felt that life could be easier. I must have recognized that I was struggling but was in no way equipped to deal with it or even explain it.

There were times we attended church, and my Mom sketched an image of Jesus on her bedroom wall. I asked her, "How do you know if you believe in God?" "Well you just know," she replied. God must have been calling me even as a young child.

Much later on in life, after salvation, I learned through God's prophets that there was an event that happened as early as age three where I was touched sexually. This event happened at an age that I cannot remember, and I had already begun to develop same-sex attraction and lust at age five. Obviously, I didn't know what to do about it, so I kept this secretly bottled up and buried deep inside. I was always very quiet and struggled to connect with most kids. I didn't always have a playground buddy to race out to recess with. I just felt so different and unacceptable, but again didn't have the language to express or explain how I felt, so I was really left in a state of confusion.

I struggled to keep up with the other kids in school, and in kindergarten and first grade, my teachers suggested I be held back. However, I was reluctant to keep going forward. I would get lost in my imagination and find myself daydreaming in classes. In the third grade, I was diagnosed with an Attention Deficit Disorder. There were some attempts to aim me in the right direction, but people who were supposed to be there to provide counsel and guidance failed me when I needed them to step in the most. People typically don't put their whole heart into things and will fail you at very critical times in your life. A fleshly mind wouldn't have been able to figure out the root cause anyway because it was hiding in the spirit realm all along. A lot of people prayed but very few of them prayed enough to get deep revelations from God that would have brought the prophetic counsel and deliverance that I so needed in my life.

Around age ten, I joined boy scouts and made a group of friends. We had sleepovers and played together like normal kids. I had a very difficult time coming out of my shell. Because I had these feelings of being unaccepted, it was very hard for me to come out of my shell. I was always so afraid to just open up and was very closed off for the most part. I had some very strong boundaries that stayed with me all the time. I wanted so badly to be able to open up, but just couldn't. My friends and I would go roller skating at the local skating rink almost every weekend. I even had a girlfriend here and there, but never went steady with any of them. By the time I made it to high school, we had all grown apart and became more involved with different groups of friends.

CHAPTER 2

Destructive Adolescence

At age fourteen, I experimented with marijuana for the first time. Some friends picked me up, and we smoked until it was time for me to go home. They told me that some people can't get high the first time they smoke, but I was determined to find out what it was like so I just kept smoking and smoking. When we arrived at my house to drop me off, I stepped out of the car and then it finally hit me and it hit me hard. I was messed up from the floor up, which was where I spent the next few hours. I was so stoned I couldn't walk. But that didn't stop me from trying it again and again and again. I also started drinking and smoking cigarettes. Pretty soon, all the people that I hung around with at least smoked cigarettes and drank from time to time.

A few of my friends and I had three wheelers and four wheelers and would spend a lot of time riding around on the gravel roads. We'd sometimes sneak off to cemeteries and such to smoke cigarettes, and if we could get our hands on it, we would drink and smoke weed. We could ride to one another's homes without ever getting off those gravel roads. Sometimes we'd find someone to buy us alcohol, and we'd go to each other's homes to drink or get stoned while our parents were working. The only time I really felt normal was when I got messed up. Drugs and alcohol were the addictive substances that helped me connect with others and helped me to open up and have fun. To me, at the time, I was just having fun; but in all truth, I was subconsciously escaping how I felt on the inside.

My secret sexual struggle was unbearable; no one knew of the pain and fear that I carried around deep inside. I asked God to change my sexuality, but nothing ever transpired from it at that time. I felt so scared and hopeless, and often wondered what would become of my life. I had no trustworthy person I could turn to, and even if I did, it seemed no one would have the right answers to my predicament. I had a huge fear of anyone finding out so it was impossible to seek help. I feared their reaction would be disgust and rejection. I remember sitting on the end of my bed with a gun to my head wishing I could just end the misery of all that I was dealing with, but I knew I couldn't do it. I developed a lot of deep emotional wounds, and drugs and alcohol were the self-destructive ways I used to cope with life. Getting messed up was a destructive way of comforting and loving myself, and it was also a way to escape how I felt about myself. I battled suicidal thoughts off and on throughout different parts of my life. I wasn't a feminine person, so most people had no idea what was going on inside me. I still had no desire to be female, but I struggled with same-sex attraction. I was confused and had no one to turn to. I was desperate for help, but too afraid of being exposed. Throughout my adolescence, drinking and drug use progressed.

In a smaller town, there isn't much to do. On the weekends, if there wasn't a party going on, we'd all pile in vehicles, and cruise around on gravel roads drinking and smoking ourselves stupid. By the time I graduated high school, I had been busted for underage drinking a few times. One night, I had a couple friends in my car with me cruising around drinking and ended up in a head-on collision with another drunk driver, which totaled out both vehicles involved. We all went to jail that night, and I received my first DUI. I walked through my high school graduation with my face cut up from being thrown into the front windshield of my car. As bad as it was, I was actually kind of proud of that. The consequences were not exactly easy to deal with though. I was without a car for a while and was placed on supervised probation.

Still, I was not convinced that my drinking was a problem and continued on with the party life. To me, I was just having fun, but to everyone else, I had a drinking problem. Before that first year of probation was up, I was arrested again for underage drinking. My probation officer gave me six weeks of SATOP classes, yet I did not take it seriously. Before that program was over, I got another arrest for the same offense, which added another six weeks to my SATOP program. Sadly, before I could finish the program, I was busted yet again for drinking. I felt doomed as I had to face the toughest probation officer in the county. Knowing she would probably send me to do jail time at this point, I admitted to her that I felt I had a problem and that I wanted to go to rehab. In my mind, this was really a plan to keep myself from having to spend time in jail and my employer allowed me this time off.

The Judge added another year to my probation and ordered me to complete the rehab program followed with a three-month outpatient SATOP program. The program helped to see that I had a problem and taught me the basics about addictions. I was also exposed to a lot of different people who had been in a lot more trouble and facing harsher judgments from the courts, which helped me to see that I had to buckle down and make a decision. Either I could sober up and eventually get out of all this mess, or I could continue down this dead-end road that led to prison or death. After completing all the programs, which ended up being approximately seven months all together, I stayed sober from alcohol for a couple years. I had other friends who were in the same type of trouble.

I completed all the sobriety programs as well as probation, but before that period of probation ended, I became hooked on methamphetamine around age twenty, yet somehow flew under my probation officer's radar. I was so messed up that I was constantly late for work if I even showed up at all. Eventually, I just quit that job and stayed high all the time. I knew the drug had a serious hold on me and remember asking God to deliver me from it. Not long after that, the main drug dealer got busted and went to prison. It's funny how we tend to pray at critical moments in life, but when God answers, we go on with life as if it probably would have happened anyway, basically forgetting we ever even prayed until later on in life when God begins to bring these moments back to the surface of our minds. That's when we can truly see the footprints in the sand to see that Jesus was with us all along. Meth became harder and harder to get around that time and I slowed down enough to get my life back in order. I got a job working in a factory building lawn mower engines and was able to save up enough money to buy furniture and move into my first apartment. I moved to a larger town, Poplar Bluff, which is where I worked and wasn't far from my hometown. It was the first time having my own place, and I loved having my independence. Finally, for the first time, life seemed to be balanced. A friend asked me to take her to her senior prom. We went to prom together then went to the after-party, which is where I ended my two years of sobriety and began drinking regularly again.

I can say I've always looked at life and saw it as a journey to find meaning and understanding of what this life is about. Have you ever stopped to think and asked yourself, why am I here? Why am I in this body and why are we here on this planet? The first time I felt God calling me, I was twenty-one years of age. That's the age most adolescents get excited about because then they can legally buy alcohol. However, I felt the call of God and decided to find a church. It was like my attention was suddenly drawn to God for no apparent reason at all. I remember driving through town on the main business strip and just looking around when I saw the very church that I ended up going into. It was a Baptist church close to where I lived, just off the main drag. I went by myself, and it was a bit strange and awkward. I can't say I remember any of the sermons, but I went up to get saved. The Pastor sent me into a room with some other man, probably a deacon of the church, to discuss being saved. Basically, the understanding I remember getting from it was that if a person believes Jesus died on the cross for their sins, and confesses Jesus Christ as their Lord and Savior, they are saved. I was disappointed and confused that it wasn't a more powerful experience. I didn't feel the presence or power of God.

Looking back, I know I felt the call of God, but wasn't able to truly receive salvation because I didn't know and understand that Jesus died for my sins because I had no reason to believe that other than someone saying so. Also, I wasn't truly ready to lay my life down. I didn't know anything about the Holy Spirit at that time, and I definitely did not realize how powerful it could be. However, I went on with it and decided to get baptized, but I was not "born again." Unfortunately, this was short-lived. Consumed by the excitement of experiencing more of the party life, I said, "God, I'm just not ready yet." And I went right back into my lifestyle like nothing ever happened. I allowed myself to forget all about God. I wanted to forget. God doesn't forget though. He didn't give up on me either, although I dismissed Him so easily. I didn't last two months in church, but God had a plan all along. I just didn't realize it until almost nine years later, but during that time, I was turned over to a reprobate mind; so much so that the memory of this brief period of "almost-salvation" was blotted from my mind like it never happened.

I slipped right back into my lifestyle, which at that time consisted of partying with friends, drinking, popping pills, occasionally smoking pot, and basically indulging in anything else we could get our hands on. That went on for a few years, and Jenny and I became friends. I think we were impressed with one another's ability to party all night long more than an actual attraction. Long story short, we ended up pregnant when I was twenty-three years old. We moved in together and thought maybe we could sober up and make it work. I found myself feeling very trapped and was still secretly struggling with same-sex attractions.

Still, no one knew about this and I desperately wanted to be free so that I could finally live out the life of this person I kept hidden on the inside for so many years. Three months after our daughter was born, Jenny and I realized we weren't going to be happy together. I was unhappy and so naturally she became unhappy too. A few months after my daughter was born, Jenny asked me a terrifying question, "Are you happy?" I remember how scared and alone I felt when I had to tell her the truth. The answer was no. I was freaking out on the inside because I knew I couldn't live my life pretending and trying to force myself to be something that I wasn't. Although she wasn't happy either, I'm sure she at least felt the same empty, scared, and lonely feelings. I moved out the very next day.

CHAPTER 3

Where do I belong in life

About a month or so later, I felt like I needed to be honest with Jenny about why things did not work out. I told her I was gay, and that was why I was so unhappy. That didn't make things any better considering our newborn child, if you can imagine, but it was time to bring some understanding into the picture and just be honest. By that time, I had already started frequenting gay bars in a town about an hour away from my hometown.

I was so desperate to find myself and to be who I felt I was on the inside all along, and life seemed to be pushing me in that direction. I became a very selfish person. I gave up fighting against the flesh and decided to openly embrace homosexuality as my identity. I ripped myself out of my daughters' life and ran away from all of it, but not one day went by that I didn't think about my daughter. When there is another life that is connected to you, you just never forget. The thought of God or prayer during these years was as far from me as the east is to the west. The only person I was interested in finding was myself, and there wasn't anything or anyone that could change that. I remember a conversation I had with my Mother right before I moved away. I said, "Mom, don't you think there's more to life than this small-town life?" She said, "Well, what do you think is out there?" "I don't know, but I'm going to find out," I replied. I can only imagine how that must have ripped her heart out to see what was happening and knew nothing could stop it. She said, "Well, it's your life and you have to live it."

As tension grew between Jenny and myself, I stopped seeing my daughter. I just wanted to escape it all, so that's what I did. I never had a chance to be who I felt I was on the inside, and I didn't understand how to be a Father. Being in a small town, I felt the only way that I was going to be able to be happy was to stop hiding inside myself, yet the only way I felt comfortable "coming out" was to run away because I felt very exposed, scared, ashamed, yet relieved at the same time. The secret I kept hidden my entire life, up to that moment, was out. I ended up meeting Tom, and very quickly moved to a larger town that was about an hour drive away from my hometown. Life as I knew it was drastically changing very quickly.

At last, for the first time, I was experiencing life in a way that felt so fresh, so new, so exciting. I felt fulfilled by the excitement and newness of life. Finally, I was able to meet people in a community where I didn't have to feel ashamed or even have to hide who I was. I started working out and eating healthy, so I was getting all the attention I needed to boost my ego. For the first time in my life, I had confidence. The relationship with Tom was great. We were both very active and stayed fit. We spent a lot of time outdoors riding bikes and hiking. We also frequented the local bars, wineries, festivals, and dined out often at some rather nice places. I felt I was in love, and the feelings that developed were strong.

Today, looking back, I can see I was desperate to feel loved, which made it easy to fall in love with someone. That type of love does not last though because it is based on vulnerability caused by the lack of acceptance, love and affection in life; and it is driven by a spirit of lust. Lust creates a false sense of love. I had a big empty void in my soul that needed to be filled, although at the time I did not identify a void. At the time, I just needed to find that special person that would make me whole; not much different from anyone else, be it gay or straight.

Tom was older than me and very settled in his lifestyle. However, for me, life seemed to be just beginning, and those feelings faded. I was becoming more and more interested in other people and places. Suddenly, after being in the relationship for one year, those intense feelings of what I thought were love faded away and selfish pride ruled my life. Suddenly, the relationship still wasn't enough for me, and I wanted to venture out into the world a little further, at the cost of breaking yet another heart. I was not ready to be settled the way that Tom was and still had a lot of discovering to do. I was hungry for more and more of whatever this world had to offer, and eager to explore my life to find out what it was I was really after. We broke up, and I moved out of Tom's house and into a small apartment.

CHAPTER 4

Meandering Further into the World

I began going on social media to find connections in other places, particularly St. Louis. I have always been an introverted person, yet I was fearless and enjoyed the adventure and excitement as I merged into life in the fast lane. After learning a little bit about the city, I ended up driving up to meet some friends. That night, I met Mark. He approached me and handed me a business card with his number. The night life and bar scene soon became my new atmosphere. I finally found a place where there was enough excitement to keep my attention. I think I was extremely bored with life, and this was very stimulating to me in many ways compared to what I was used to. I was experiencing a life I could only imagine from back home. I didn't have to hide myself, and it felt good for the first time in my life. I felt so free and liberated. I looked good, and in that scene, that was all I needed to make it. At last, I found a place where I seemed to fit. I enjoyed the night life there, and there was always something going on in the city.

I started contacting Mark, who had a fun outgoing personality. I wasn't actually looking for a relationship, but we developed those same intense feelings of love, and hit it off very quickly. Mark owned his own pool company, owned a very nice house in an upscale neighborhood, drove nice cars and always seemed to have plenty of money. Everything seemed to be so conveniently at my fingertips. We dated for a couple months, and then I was able to put in a transfer with my job and transferred to St. Louis. Within another month or so, I moved in with Mark. I found myself in a whole new world. We had lots of friends and went to lots of fun pool parties. We were always going out to expensive upscale dining and going out for drinks with friends. I felt like I had found what I was looking for; at last, it was what I had been missing my whole life. The exciting new lifestyle seemed to have swept me off my feet.

It didn't take long for Mark's demons to start coming out of the closet. I was beginning to see who Mark really was but was so wrapped up in this lifestyle that I ended up being passive and even in denial about things. We both had a history of hard drug use. He still dabbled from time to time, and soon I began to dabble in it again too. I had been clean and sober for a couple years at this point. Drugs always seemed to trigger a totally different side of Mark. I could tell Mark was not in control, and that was probably the part that made me more uncomfortable than anything. Our problems ended up being a vicious cycle that would circle back around continuously. I endured this emotional roller coaster for a couple of years. What started out great turned into an extremely emotionally unhealthy relationship that I needed to get out of. The material things no longer mattered. I had everything, yet I had nothing. The financial security, all the nice cars and upscale neighborhood didn't matter to me anymore. I had to get out! I had to take legal action to sever the tie with this person.

I ended up finding a job and rented a bedroom from a friend. He was an older man who had a lot of problems of his own. During that period that I stayed at his house, I literally watched his life deteriorate and saw him hit rock bottom due to alcoholism. On top of that, he was very diabetic and was losing feeling in his feet. It wasn't uncommon for him to stumble or fall down the stairs, or even to find him passed out from drinking with low blood sugar. This man was a successful pharmacy manager at a very reputable hospital for many years, but he ended up losing his job and had to move in with his parents when he got so bad that he could not take care of himself anymore. It is really sad how the evil in this world works to corrupt lives and destroy souls. I ended up moving out and renting my own place, and then I met Kyle.

I went through yet another bad relationship that wreaked havoc on my life. Basically, every situation seemed to go from good to bad to worse, and this was the worst. Long story short, the gay lifestyle started out great, but as time went on, things got worse and worse. It never got better; it only got darker. A lot darker! I made it to a point in life where I lost hope to find lasting happiness and became very vulnerable to addiction. Suddenly, meth and other hard drugs had such a hold on me that I could not break free. I was no longer in control of my life.

I had this dream where I was walking down a street during the day time. As I walked down the street, I saw a cave to my left. The opening was big and dark. I entered into this dark cave, which tunneled below street level for a long distance. Upon entering, I noticed a man standing against the right side, who I knew as Christian in real life from back home. I tried to speak to him, but it was as if he couldn't see me or hear me. To my left, there was an area with a black piano. I went further and further down the path of this dark underground place. Suddenly, I had a small group of other young men with me and we were being chased by some "bad guys" that were tracking us.

We were running for our lives as we were being chased deeper and deeper into this dark tunnel. This tunnel seemed to become more and more narrow making it difficult to travel down. I came to a hiding place that appeared to be a short wood partition like a horse stable, so I jumped behind it to hide from these men that were chasing us. I hunched down fearing that I would be seen. The group of young men that were with me continued running deeper into the tunnel, and we were separated at that point. From inside the stall, I could hear the running footsteps and movement of these men who were tracking us. I could also see beams of sunlight shining in through between the boards of the stall wall and saw the feet of these men who were tracking us pass by me. Quickly, I turned and ran back the way that I came and made it out of the dark cave. On my way out of the cave, to my right, the man that I saw at the beginning was playing the piano.

Before I moved out of that apartment, I spoke to a neighbor that lived right beside me and I felt at liberty to share the dream I had with him. He told me that I would end up going back to something that I had done before. I didn't know what he meant by that, but he assured me that it would not be a bad thing. I had no idea that the dream was from God. I didn't even know that God spoke to people through dreams at that point, so to me, it was just a bizarre dream. Was God speaking to me and I didn't know? In the next chapters, you'll see how life unfolded to reflect this dream.

I believe He speaks to many of us through dreams, but we simply don't pay attention. We are usually too quick to dismiss a dream that seems odd or bizarre, but I believe we should take dreams more serious especially if the dream is vivid or stands out. I encourage people to write down their dreams, pray for the meaning, and examine the details even if you don't understand the dreams. They often become words of knowledge and confirmations later on to help you know you are on the right track and that God is with you through the darkness and the light. Often, they are a reflection of situations and turning points in our lives and when things transpire later on, we can look back and see the footprints of Jesus where he was leading us and we didn't even know it.

I ended up moving into a new apartment in a different neighborhood right after Kyle left. I just wanted to start over and forget about all of it. We've all been there and needed a fresh start after a bad experience. It was like I was holding it together well enough that no one really had any idea I was hanging on by a thread. I just knew I had to keep going, and surely at some point, life would unfold something good again.

CHAPTER 5

Glimmers of Light in Utter Darkness

I went to a counselor hoping to find some kind of direction for my life, but he just listened and didn't offer any suggestions. Not that I ever asked for any suggestions nor did I realize at that time that was really why I was seeking counsel. Whether I realized it at the time or not, I was seeking direction and guidance. It was like my inner soul was searching, but in the natural, I didn't have clarity; my inner man was searching, but I was lost. So, counseling seemed to be another dead end. I didn't know what to do with my life. I was tired of meandering through life, but I had no real plan. I guess you could say aimlessness was my approach to life; roll the dice and see what hand you get this time. I needed a vacation to escape my problems, and meth took me on a long vacation. I had always been able to manage my drug use for the most part, and I had done my share of heavy drinking throughout the years but after a few rough years of heartaches, I became more vulnerable and susceptible to the addictions. Suddenly, crystal meth took a hold of my life, and I found myself chemically addicted and spiraling down faster than ever. It didn't take long to become chemically addicted and was partying all the time. Eventually, I found myself trying to quit and tried several times but could not shake it. So, I did what we all do when we can't change something about ourselves, I accepted it and it became part of who I was. I accepted it as part of my lifestyle. My looks changed as I lost a lot of weight, my hair became thin, and my skin color changed. I was looking like death and it did not take long to get there. I stopped going out to bars and surrounded myself with all sorts of different people who were involved in the drug scene. Some were obviously drug dealers, all were drug addicted, and some were even secretly into various forms of witchcraft. Meth seemed to open me up to a whole different realm of things; another dimension of life.

My life was deteriorating rapidly. One day, as I stood in the kitchen of my apartment pondering where my life was headed, I could see that things were only going to get worse and worse. I remember looking down and seeing this dark tunnel open up in front of me and seeing myself spiraling further and further down into it. I was afraid of where I saw life taking me. I said, "God, if you are real, show me." I thought it was odd that I said that and thought to myself, "Why did I say that?" It was barely a month or so later when God answered. I had basically forgotten that I had made a request. I wasn't expecting anything, and it wasn't even in my thoughts of searching.

One day, I was out riding my bike in the neighborhood near where I lived and had stopped to grab lunch. I sat there trying to eat the sandwich I had just bought, but I couldn't as these emotions became too much to hold back from crying in public. I bagged up my lunch and quickly rode home on my bike. I rushed into the back door of my apartment, and I just lost it. There I was in my kitchen yet again. I thought it was interesting when I learned that the kitchen in the prophetic context represents a place of preparation. I erupted in emotion crying like I had never cried before. On that day, in that moment, there was an unveiling where I was discerning and recognizing the fallen nature of the world like I had never recognized it before. From the floor, I looked up noticing the room was lit differently. The walls of my apartment where white, but I was seeing it lit in a yellowish light. I began to have this vision, and in it seeing all the people I had surrounded myself with; the homosexuals, drug addicts and dealers, different types of perversion, and different forms of witchcraft.

All of these, God was showing me, as they circled in front of me one by one, I saw that there had been things such as abuse, molestation, rape, rejection, abandonment, lack of love and affection from parents and all sorts of events that the world had inflicted upon them that wounded them early on in their lives, which in turn had shaped them into those destructive lifestyles. Then I saw myself and the Lord said to me, "You are not living to be what I created you to be." Then I saw Jesus on the cross, and He said, "Who will save them for they know not what they do?" After the vision, comfort and peace descended upon me, and I got up off the floor. I really was not sure of what just happened to me.

At that point, I didn't know whether it was my imagination or not, but I just remember thinking that as time unfolds, I would know. When I had that encounter with God, suddenly I was able to believe and because I was able to believe in my heart, I was able to receive Him into my life. When it is all said and done, I was really on a journey through life seeking truth and the meaning of life all along. It was like suddenly, I had just walked right into the Door of Truth face first and as time went on, I began walking through that door and was translated from darkness to light as I began calling Him Lord. However, I was still in darkness for a little while longer. You can see that this is where I was in the dream where I hid behind the wall. The beam of light that shown through the boards as the enemy ran past me represented this encounter with the Holy Spirit within the vision, and when I turned and headed back the way I came, that means I was on my way out of the jaws of Hell and being restored to Christ. However, I still had a little way to go before I made it completely out of the mouth of Hell. In the dream, the dark underground tunnel was the path that leads to Hell.

I remained chemically dependent on drugs for a while after that, but knew God was leading me and became more aware of His presence over time. I found myself coming into communion late at night and at different times where I would have these encounters with the Holy Spirit and He would minister to me as to why I was the way I was. It was the still small voice of our Heavenly Father. I knew I had lived a life of confusion, gay or not gay, because of the revelation I had reveals what this world really is, which is fallen. We are all going in all sorts of directions out of our fallen fleshly nature until God intervenes with an unveiling that leads us into all truth. God pierced the veil, and I was able to begin to see things under a new Light, a light of Truth. When I walked through that Door, I found that on the other side of it was an abundance of truth, love, forgiveness, healing, grace, joy, purpose, righteousness, and spiritual warfare.... but behind me on the other side of it was a world of darkness, confusion, deception, lies, betrayal and pain. I was able to discern things more and more as time went on.

As much as my flesh didn't want to change, my heart simply could not go back to living in deception. I was discerning the dark cloud of confusion that lingers upon the earth and how it affects people's ability to see the truth, know the truth, and receive the truth. People are blind until God intervenes. People don't know the truth even when it's right in front of them because the enemy has them blinded. Jesus is the Way, the Truth, and the Life. We are born out of darkness and transformed by the Light into light. After my encounter, I was spiritually awakened. Life as I knew it would never be the same though it took me some time to get all the way through the door.

Hebrews 10:20 says, "By a new and living way, which he hath consecrated for us, through the veil, that is to say, his flesh."

Ephesians 5:13-14 NIV says, "But everything exposed by the light becomes visible-and everything that is illuminated becomes a light. This is why it is said: 'Wake up, sleeper, rise from the dead, and Christ will shine upon you.'"

I remained drug addicted for a while after that, but knew God was leading me. I tried to quit the habit at different times but couldn't in my own strength. Could God have just delivered me right then and there? Yes, He could have, but He was still using my situation to expose the darkness of this world. I remember one prayer that I prayed continually during this time in my life. "God, let your truth unfold in my life." I didn't know how or when I would be delivered from drug addiction, but I knew God was going to deliver me.

CHAPTER 6

Rescued out of the Mouth of Hell

As I mentioned before, meth seemed to open me up to a different realm. Later on, I learned that drugs are used in certain occult practices for the very purpose of opening themselves up to experiencing more of the spirit realm. Drugs are used in sorcery, black magic, casting spells as well as various other occult practices. I knew several warlocks, sorcerers and witches, however they never confessed to be such and their practices were mostly done in secret. I was oblivious to it at the time and all I know is things sure got strange as Satan sent his servants into my life to deceive me with things that were contrary to what the

Holy Spirit Himself told me. Beelzebub, also known as lord of flies

Zeek was a friend I had connections with to get drugs, whom I met after I had the vision. We used to get high and talk about God a lot. One night, as we stood in my living room talking, I noticed something moving around the lamp across the room. What I saw was some sort of particles floating and swirling around the lit fixtures of a vintage floor lamp I had placed by a wall in my living room. As I gazed across the room at it, I said, "Zeek, do you see that?" "Yes," he replied. Then there was what looked like a big black housefly flying from the lamp at one end of the apartment to the other, flying back and forth between us as we stood there talking. "Is that a fly," I asked? Both of us realizing that it was thirty degrees and freezing outside so we determined the answer was no. It was bigger than a housefly around the size of a dime or nickel but was black and mimicked a fly in appearance and in the pattern in which it flew.

We continued talking in amazement of what we were seeing as this golden yellowish mist began to form, which was much more concentrated at the corner of the ceiling and the wall. "What is this," I asked? Zeek replied, "It's our angels, and they are excited that we are talking about this." He was impressed that I was able to see this phenomenon. He said, "Most people cannot see this, and that I was one of the few that could." He encouraged me to reach up and touch it. He told me that if I would reach up with my hand that they would reach down and touch me back with theirs. No, I wasn't comfortable with that so he did it first. He reached up towards this mist with his hand

and when he did, his hand lit up around the edges glowing with heat waves coming off of it. It was getting late and Zeek finally left, but this was something that seemed to happen often when he was around during this time.

2 Corinthians 11:14-15 says "And no marvel; for Satan himself is transformed into an angel of light. Therefore it is no great thing if his ministers also be transformed as the ministers of righteousness; whose end shall be according to their works."

Zeek seemed to know a lot about the Bible and would quote things that were supposed to be from the Bible as we were talking, but at that time, I knew absolutely nothing about the word of God to be able to say whether or not his quotations were true. Zeek would act like he knew God, but at the same time would be trying to persuade me to believe that God did not care if I used drugs and that when Jesus died on the cross for our sins so we were forgiven as long as we believed in Him. He would try to lead people to believe that they could live life however we wished and as long as we believed, then we were saved from Hell. He was a sorcerer who operated in the realm of black magic and divination. A lot of strange things would happen during his visits.

As we sat there in my living room talking one night, taking notice of a small crinkled piece of paper near our feet, suddenly it shifted across the floor several inches. Zeek asked, "Did you see that?" As I looked down to see what he was talking about, I saw it move a few inches across the floor, and then as we observed this happening, we could see this crinkled piece of paper just sort of trembling on the hardwood floor of my apartment.

That same night, we saw flashes of light on the walls. These flashes were like that of a camera flash, only not as bright and seemed to appear in random sizes and shapes.

One day, during the afternoon, I was home alone and had decided to lay down on the couch for a nap and as I was waking up, I felt a claw gently move across the left side of my forehead. As my eyes opened, I saw a shadow move from my left side. Later on that day, when I told Zeek what I had experienced, he suggested that it was my guardian angel. But I knew this was a dark presence. Later on, visiting a friends' house, there was an older man there with whom I had a conversation. He told me a story about a witch who had a Celtic knot tattoo on her back and that a black shadow figure leaped out of the tattoo and into an infant. He said he panicked for the baby and could hardly talk. Many strange occurrences were happening, but I believe God was allowing me to experience things to make me more aware of what is going on around us in the spirit realm and expose the works of darkness in the world.

Another night as we were standing in my apartment talking, the golden yellowish mist began to form again. It was similar to the mist that would form from a hot shower only this had a color and made the air appear very fluid. Zeek described it as "soupy." While we were standing there, something came down out of the atmosphere and touched my shirt. We both saw something like a rod come straight down out of the atmosphere and gently poke my shirt on my right side just under my chest. We even saw my shirt move when it poked me. It was as if a ghost came up and poked me. That's the best way I could describe this but both of us were seeing all of these manifestations. Meth is a stimulant drug that heightens all of your senses and you can actually hear sounds that you couldn't normally hear and you can see things in the spirit realm that you wouldn't normally be able to see. At least that was my experience with it. Zeek assured me these were our "guardian angels."

As time went on, I found myself coming into communion with the Holy Spirit on my own and He was revealing things to me as to why I was the way that I was. Sometimes when God speaks it's like He just speaks right into your understanding so that when He speaks the understanding simply manifest in your mind without actually audibly hearing Him. It's like a transferring of information without audibly speaking. Discerning what God is saying is a form of hearing Him. It's amazing what the Lord does. As tears streamed down my face, He was revealing to me how not having my father present in my childhood had affected me in life. It caused a major imbalance in me because of the empty void in my soul, which led to a combination of related problems. Growing up without the love of a father figure can cause boys to grow up craving love from other boys or men and can lead to sexual confusion especially if sexual abuse has occurred—not always, but it can.

To me, it seems that sexual confusion begins when two things are in place: when the father's love is removed, and when the child ends up being sexually activated by someone of the same sex whether this ends up being an adult or another child. This is how homosexuality often begins. In many cases little boys are being sexually activated by other little boys who have been touched. The thing is, little boys will never tell you what has happened and secret lustful desires begin to manifest in these innocent little children. The same thing happens with little girls and they end up being very promiscuous. At the root of all of this is the absence of love.

As I sat there in my apartment as the Holy Spirit ministered to me, I found myself weeping as He revealed the answers to my questions by speaking directly into my understanding. There was no mist, no flying black dots, and no strange movements in the atmosphere, just a still small voice and a discernible warm, comforting presence of love from the Holy Spirit. From a dark place in life, I was beginning to see glimpses of light shining through. These intimate moments with the Holy Spirit were represented as beams of light in the dream which was my turning point. Once you encounter the love of God, it changes you and you'll never be the same.

One night, I was looking to score and had contacted one of my drug dealers, who was staying in a hotel and he had invited me up. When I arrived, there were a couple people there, so I went into the restroom. Before I was even finished in the restroom, there was a knock on the door. Someone said, "Matt, come out the cops are here." "Yeah right," I replied thinking it was a joke. "No, you really need to come out." And sure enough, when I came out, there was a cop with a gun who said that they had been observing drug trafficking going on from another high-rise hotel across the way. A guy had knocked on the door looking for drugs and came in right before this so-called cop did. This "cop" interrogated us at gunpoint and searched everything in the room. The drug dealer and the guy who came in right before the cop were both sitting on the couch and I was sitting in a chair across from them.

As we sat there at gunpoint, these guys were literally manifesting demons right in front of me. I just sat there calm and quiet. I was a little bit scared but mostly knew I was going to be okay and waited for it all to be over. The cop was interrogating and questioning these guys pretty hard. He especially gave the drug dealer a hard time and said he had heard all about him and what he was about. The drug dealer's face was white as a ghost; he couldn't sit still, as he was standing up uncontrollably, with strange body movements, as this so called cop interrogated him about giving children date rape drugs and then raping them. Jesus warns us it will be as it was in the days of Noah and Lot.

Luke 17:26-30 says, "And as it was in the days of Noah, so shall it be also in the days of the Son of man. They did eat, they drank, they married wives, they were given in marriage, until the day that Noah entered into the ark, and the flood came, and destroyed them all. Likewise also as it was in the days of Lot; they did eat, they drank, they bought, they sold, they planted, they builded; But the same day that Lot went out of Sodom it rained fire and brimstone from heaven, and destroyed them all. Even thus shall it be in the day when the Son of man is revealed."

Matthew 24:12 says, "And because iniquity shall abound, the love of many shall wax cold."

The other guy kept rising up out of his seat and hissing like a venomous snake. The cop looked at me and asked, "Why aren't you freaking out like they are?" "Because I haven't done anything," I replied, which was true and I was completely sober. The roads were bad from an ice storm, which prevented me from even being able to get to an ATM to withdraw money. I had simply been guilty of bad intentions and ended up in a really ugly situation, sober and empty-handed. He literally tore the place apart and made us lay face down on the floor. He said, if we complied, there wouldn't be any consequences. When he left, he took all the electronics—a laptop, iPad, and both of our cell phones—including our wallets, all the money that was there, and all of the drugs. When they left, we knew we had just been robbed, but that guy had his act down. It was a crazy situation to end up in and these guys were professional thieves that obviously had done this a time or two. God definitely had His hands on me through all of this.

The devil should have killed me when he had the chance, but I was protected even then. God doesn't look at us the way we look at ourselves. He looks at us as a finished product, but He also looks at our heart. He searches the heart to know what's hidden there. He knows more about what's in you and what you are capable of than you do for yourself. I didn't know I had it in me to be a Christian. He looks beyond where we are and by grace He takes us to our purpose and destiny. 2 Timothy 1:9 says, "Who hath saved us, and called us with an holy calling, not according to our works, but according to his own purpose and grace, which was given us in Christ Jesus before the world began."

One night, Zeek was over and we were talking about the ability to resist sickness. He told me that to resist sickness, you simply say, "I resist sickness in the name of Jesus." He went on to tell me that he had been resisting sickness all day as he had been feeling something in his throat. I was sitting across the room from him probably six or seven feet away and as we drifted into other conversations, suddenly he coughed into his hand and this big dark black tarnish-looking (so dark black that it was as if you could see into it) lougy stuck to the palm of his hand. Zeek was a talker and so he was just holding his hand up in the air because he thought there was mucus on it while he finished talking. Then he looked at his hand, pointed at it and said, "What is that?!" "Uhhh, I don't know," I responded, but in my mind, I was thinking he must live in a pretty unclean environment. He totally did live in a pretty dirty place with lots of different stuff being smoked there. But this was not some ordinary mucus! This was actually a demon that came out by the way of resisting sickness in the name of Jesus! It was so dark that you could almost see into it. It was a deep black that almost looked like tar if you can imagine.

Zeek got up and went into the bathroom and washed his hands. He came back like nothing strange had happened and continued talking. All of a sudden, I started noticing the whole color part of his eyes was dark black and there appeared to be something dark black moving around in a circular motion in both of his eyes. He said, "Matt, you have the eyes of an angel" and began to talk about the eyes being the windows to the soul. He told me that my eyes had opened up to him. Obviously, his soul had been darkened, and this dude was crawling with demons!

One night, as we stood talking in my apartment living room, there was a big mirror which was built into the wall at the other end of the room. As we were talking, I was noticing myself in the mirror and was commenting on how bad I looked. Before meth addiction, I was fit and attractive. People used to ask me if I were a model. Drugs certainly took its toll on me. As I looked back at myself in the mirror, my image appeared seemingly worse and worse. Each time I looked back into the mirror, my skin appeared increasingly grey and my posture appeared worse and worse. Even my face seemed to be shrinking up, and I began to look hunched over like an old man. Zeek told me then that it was an illusion caused by the enemy and not to pay attention to it. He told me the enemy was trying to trick my mind.

When I looked towards Zeek and then back towards the mirror, I could literally feel my face changing or morphing. He kept telling me I didn't look bad, but what I was seeing in the mirror was pretty horrible. That's probably what I would have looked like if I had decided to reject God to continue going down that path. Thank you, Lord, for saving me! The dark tunnel I dreamed about represented this darkness and the Holy Spirit was the glimmers of light that changed my direction. It was a path that would have ultimately led to eternal damnation in Hell, and the beam of light that shone through represented God's voice that intervened and caused me to turn back and eventually find my way back out of the darkness. I believe God intervened at a time that would determine whether I would live or die. Nothing else in this world would have saved me.

Another friend of mine, Claud would come over from time to time to hang out and get high. He had a rather bizarre story about how a thick black hair came out of the screen of his iPad and entered into his eye. He said this was a demon. He also talked about how his parents thought he was dead for several years while he lived on an island somewhere. According to him, he overdosed on drugs and was taken away to live on an island. He even showed me pictures of this place. He used to talk about black magic and how the enemy speaks things over us from the spirit realm to hinder us, which is true. When the enemy speaks things to us in the spirit realm, the things they speak penetrate into our minds and if we are not discerning, we receive those as our own thoughts. He came over to visit one evening and was talking about static electricity as some sort of gift that he claimed to have. I got up to go use the restroom and as I walked across the room toward the bathroom, I walked through an invisible cloud of static energy that covered me from head to toe. He studied Toltec Shamanism by which he believed in being able to channel and control energy and reach a place called totality. He was another one of Satan's followers who was sent to deceive me. Satan knew I had heard from God and was trying everything to take what God had given me and confuse it with worldly New Age and Shamanism beliefs, which would ultimately take my idea of God and turn it into something else. It didn't work.

Claud came over one day and was talking about the technology that enabled people to be able to beam themselves from place to place. Then he showed me where he had a microchip implanted behind his ear. This was the last thing the Lord revealed to me right before delivering me from meth addiction. I told him right then that we were not serving the same God and that he was an imposter. He left shortly after that and I never saw or heard from him again. During my final meth binge, I put about a half gram of crystal meth in my glass pipe and prayed over it. I asked God to break every curse off of it and for Him to pour His love into it. I sensed that I was nearing the end of this drug addiction.

During this time, God was allowing me to go through all of this in order to show me how real the sins and forces of darkness of this fallen world really are. I was inching closer and closer to God and knew in my heart that He was going to deliver me. To me, looking at meth and how it was made, I always think of a demon-possessed mad scientist that took the elements of the earth, cursed it, and made a demon-powered substance. Meth is a substance that was made for occultic purposes, and many people whose intentions are recreational use have no idea. Drugs are demonically powered substances, which are used in sorcery and potions.

CHAPTER 7

A Step of Faith...
Faith in Action

Somewhere in the mix of all of this, I heard the Holy Spirit speak to me and He said, "Jenny will be contacting you soon." Jenny is the mother of my beautiful daughter. I had not seen my daughter in six years and was scared of what I knew I was going to have to face. I was walking around in my apartment when I heard the Lord speak this to me, and it stopped me dead in my tracks. Instantly, I became filled with anxiety and fear about this, but I said in my heart, 'Obviously, you are pushing me to do something that I would not have the strength to do on my own, but I choose to trust you.' The fear left me as quickly as it came because I made a decision to trust the Lord. I knew that He was leading me to do the right things.

One day on my drive home from work, driving through the city traffic, the Holy Spirit spoke and said, "Take a step in faith." These words went over and over in my mind as I looked around wondering, God who is this message for? Am I supposed to yell it to those people walking or who is this message for? I thought. Then I saw myself in the rearview mirror. When I saw myself, I knew it was for me, and my heart received it. I did not have any idea what taking a step of faith looked like or what that really meant, but God knew what He was doing. A couple weeks later, the Lord put me working with a girl named, Lilly. I had never worked with her the entire time I worked there, but all day she and I talked about the Bible and about God. I was still addicted to crystal meth through all of this and remember actually falling asleep in an office chair that morning because I had been up partying for so long. I didn't have a Bible and really didn't know much about it, but I had an awareness of God. Meanwhile, the Lord was planting a seed that would soon sprout and take root.

A few days later, I felt compelled to go buy a Bible after work. I didn't even know where to get one, but I remembered seeing a book rack with Christian literature in a local pharmacy. I thought, maybe I could find a Bible there. As I entered into the parking lot, His power came washing down over me, cleansing me of every drug and alcohol addiction. I parked in a parking space weeping with tears all down my face as I knew it was God's power manifesting and setting me free. At that moment, I made a promise to God. I said, "Never again." Never again would I go back to a lifestyle of addiction.

The last thing the Lord revealed to me before delivering me was the friend who showed me the chip that was implanted behind his ear. I believe God orchestrated and used my situation to reveal the truth about the condition of our sinful Nation, and what lies beneath the surface of the earth realm; exposing what is hidden behind the veil. So, what happened next, in my mind, confirmed more of the story, as I suspected, more false religion that could possibly explain where the chip came from. It all seems to tie in together.

So, I went into the store and went directly to the book rack. They didn't have a Bible, but I believe I was exactly where God wanted me to be without a doubt. There it was, 'The Complete Guide to the Bible.' I took a v-line straight to the back of the store, grabbed it and went straight to the checkout counter. When I got to the checkout counter, the two checkout employees were standing there talking. There was no one else around, just me and the two employees. One clerk stood with a CD in her hand looking at it. The other asked her, "What is that?" She replied, "Some woman just came in off the street and said for us to watch it, it's about the church of scientology." As I laid my 'Complete Guide to the Bible' on the counter, I said, "You should just throw that in the trash, that's from the enemy." I will never forget the look on the young man's face, how he smiled and lit up as he said, "You know, I have heard that, what church do you go to?" I replied, "I have not been to church yet, but I stand for Jesus Christ."

The other employee holding this audio disc interjected, "Well you should make up your own mind." It was as though, the Lord used me in that situation to intervene in a decision they would ultimately make that would either lead them into the mouth of Hell or nudge them in the right direction so they could avoid it.

That ended up being my "step of faith." There will be times God will require you to do something out of obedience in order to be blessed. As soon as I got delivered, God used me to intervene in someone's life to destroy a trap that was being set up by the devil. All of that happened by God's orchestration, and all I had to do was have "yes" in my heart for whatever God's plan ended up being. As we yield ourselves to the Lord, life will just unfold according to His will. I was on a journey of seeking and discovering the Creator, and I am still discovering Him today.

We tend to make things so difficult sometimes by trying to figure everything out before we decide to allow it to happen by faith and by keeping a yes in our heart. I have found that God usually won't reveal all of the how's and why's to get us where He wants to take us. He's more interested in getting us to realize we can trust Him to give us instruction every step of the way, rather than giving us a detailed roadmap. He won't give you the whole map, but He will give you step-by-step direction. However, there will be little clues and signs along the way as He leads our hearts, and we make it by trusting Him no matter what the circumstances are. No matter what it looks like, we walk by faith not by sight and we trust Him all the way through. If you are like I was then, you don't have anything to lose by trusting God to be Lord over your life.

It has been said, 'It's when you have nothing left to hold onto that you learn to trust God.' The beauty of this was that I didn't have to figure out what the "step of faith" was going to be or what it was going to look like or even why I was going to be taking a step-in faith, I just had to have the desire to do His will and trust Him. Faith is something that God gives us as a gift, so if your faith is moving you, trust that faith. He led me and I ended up being exactly where He wanted me to be because He orchestrated things this way. As life unfolds, day by day, God will orchestrate many life-changing events in our lives. I had my faith engaged and my heart was willing. I was willing, and it was His timing. Hebrews 11:1 says, "Now faith is the substance of things hoped for, the evidence of things not seen."

A few weeks later, late one night, I received a text on my phone. I woke up to look at it and it was a text from Jenny asking me to pay child support. I had not heard from her since I left and moved away. I read the text and went back to sleep. The next day, I sent her a text back asking her if she ever wanted me to be part of Daughter's life. I'm sure she wanted to say no since my daughter had not seen me since she was six months old and didn't know me, but we talked on the phone and decided we would meet at a park. I could see my daughter but she was not ready to introduce me as her Dad yet, which was fine and I understood it was going to take some time. Coming back into my daughters' life was one of the hardest things I have had to face because I knew it probably wouldn't come easy. Not only did I abandon my daughter, but I rejected the father nature within me because, well, I had never seen anyone father a child, and so I had to allow the Holy Spirit to teach and guide me.

I suppose I never felt qualified as a real man up to that point in life. I had to gain my daughter's trust and her family's trust. I had to take baby steps with my daughter until she was comfortable with me and there was resistance, but no matter what came up against me, I kept choosing to trust and count on the Lord to guide me through it. He has taken care of me every step of the way, and today I am a regular part of her life, and I accept myself both as a real man and Father; I accept myself the way my Creator sees me. We have to be able to see ourselves through our Father's eyes in order to truly see who we are created to be, which only comes by spending time in His presence. Although our relationship is not perfect or the way that it should be between a daughter and father, I still know God is in control and is leading us to a place in life where we will have an unbreakable bond as He has shown me this in my dreams. Restoring this type of broken relationship is a process that can take time. I simply trust God and carry my cross knowing that God is leading us both to a place of restoration and there is no one strong enough to stop that from happening.

I reconnected with my aunt after God delivered me from meth, she was the first person to really teach me about prayer. We talked on the phone and she prayed with me. I was still living in St. Louis at the time and she was living back in my hometown where I grew up. I already started making trips down to visit my daughter, so I said to her, "Next time I'm down visiting, I want you to take me to your church."

I remember walking through those doors as we entered into the sanctuary and the face of the deacon of the church lit up at me and said, "Wow, you're gonna be alright; I can see it on your face!" I was just so excited to be there to experience more of God, which was pretty strange considering I used to say that I would never go back to a church. The Lord has used the prophetic gifts in the church to help me find my way through many of the twists and turns of life, and I am grateful to be part of such a strong church that allows the Holy Spirit to flow. I began coming every chance I got and became a member of the church. I also decided to get baptized again with a new commitment to God. It was something that really meant something to me; a new beginning and a fresh start with God. I took it very seriously as I began a process of surrendering everything to God; a process of breaking away the layers from my fleshly intellect in order to rely on the Holy Spirit, for He leads us down better paths than we can find for ourselves.

It wasn't long that I ended up making a decision to quit my job and leave my life in St. Louis to do what the Lord was leading me to do, which was to be back home with my family and more connected to the church He had chosen for me to attend. There is always opposition any time the Lord is moving you in a direction. People in the world will always say things to discourage you and break your faith during times of transition, which I can say I've experienced some of that. But it should be expected because that is the fallen nature of this world. You can't listen to the same people that you used to listen to. When you start walking by faith, people are not going to understand, but you have to allow your faith to lead you.

As a new creature in Christ, you become more spiritual, and so you will flow through circumstances by the leading of the Holy Spirit if you are going to succeed on your journey. It won't always make sense to the natural man because these things are spiritually discerned. You have to trust God wholeheartedly and not leaning on your own understanding. Learn to rely on God for every move in your life and pray for discernment that will enable you to sense the direction of the Holy Spirit in your life. Stop going to this person and that person. God wants you to learn to get it from Him. I had someone once tell me, "It's when you feel at peace with it." You have to recognize the enemy speaks through people at certain times to try to throw you off and discourage you. I knew God was leading me, and no one was going to convince me otherwise; and I had peace about it. I had to find what God was saying and forget what people were saying. People will mislead you, your own family will mislead you, but if you get in tune with the Holy Spirit, He will lead you the right way every single time.

Coworkers expressed their concerns that I was making a rash decision to move so quickly and suggested that it wouldn't be so easy to replace the good job that I had. They warned me about all the conflicting issues that my daughter's mother and I would have. I understood their concern, and although it might not be easy, I knew what I had to do. I had to pursue faith and obey whatsoever the Lord God commanded. I knew I had a calling and a destiny that I was beginning to feel from within myself that I had to get to. I was predestined for something much greater than I ever knew possible—and the same is true for you. I didn't know what it was, but I knew if I followed the leading of the

Holy Spirit, He would transform my life into something much more meaningful and beautiful than I ever imagined. There was something that God was leading me to that I had not discovered yet. I knew it in my heart, and if I had allowed people to discourage me, I never would have arrived at my God-given destiny; I never would have fulfilled my true purpose in life. I had to keep saying yes, for the promises of God are yes and amen.

"For all the promises of God are yea, and in him Amen, unto the glory of God by us." —2 Corinthians 1:20

I had to disconnect from all the friends that I had because they couldn't understand what was suddenly going on in my life. Suddenly, I had these deep convictions, and I knew I had to change. It wasn't because I didn't love or care for them, but my life was shifting in a new direction. I wasn't staying, and they sure weren't coming with me so I had to let go. As I expressed my faith to a friend, he said to me, "You know, it's okay for you to still be gay, right?" I nodded my head yes, but felt the truth convicting me in my heart. He went on to explain that he went to a church one time and when he talked to the pastor about being gay, this pastor told him basically that times have changed and evolved and that it was okay, thus leading him to believe that since the pressures are greater now days so God is going to be more lenient.

Later, I felt compelled to correct myself as not to be part of this deception, so I sent that friend a text message explaining that I no longer felt it was okay for me to live my life that way. I felt I had to speak the truth on the matter even if he wasn't going to receive it. I felt that I needed to keep my hands clean. A couple other friends wanted to see me before I left St. Louis, but most of them I didn't bother telling. I just sort of disappeared from the entire gay lifestyle all together. My life was shifting and going in a completely different direction, and no one could understand.

I went to dinner with another friend before I left the city and of course the same subject came up about diverting away from the gay lifestyle and perusing my faith. I think he was able to agree that God exists but would completely disagree with homosexuality being wrong in any way. They thought this was absurd if you can imagine. Others even suggest that it is genetic.

Jude 1:4 says, "For there are certain men crept in unawares, who were before of old ordained to this condemnation, ungodly men, turning the grace of our God into lasciviousness, and denying the only Lord God, and our Lord Jesus Christ."

Jude 1:7 says," Even as Sodom and Gomorrha, and the cities about them in like manner, giving themselves over to fornication, and going after strange flesh, are set forth for an example, suffering the vengeance of eternal fire."

Another friend had texted me a few times about coming to see me off before I left. At one point, I responded for him to come over, which of course then he wanted to know if I needed him to bring any crystal over. "Well maybe just a little for old time sake," I texted back. Suddenly, I began feeling my body longing for the drug as adrenaline was released into my body. I could not do it though; not after God had delivered me, and not after the promise that was made. I was conscious of the fact that this would be detrimental if I ended up letting this happen and so many things rushed through my mind in that moment, but I texted him back and said, "I'm sorry, but I just can't do this, we'll have to meet up another time." Resist the devil and he will flee from you. He was a very busy full-time drug dealer, so it wasn't too hard to shake him off.

As hard as it was to say no, I could not let the enemy take me back to what I came out of. I had to resist it and go forward with what God was leading me to do. For once in my life, I needed to be true to myself. The moment I did that, everything came back into focus, and I was safe from what the devil was trying to lure me into. While temptations may still come, it's when it no longer has control over you that you've truly been delivered. I also testify that I have never been tempted to use drugs ever since I resisted it that day. So, it is true, resist the devil and it will flee from you. Temptations, no matter how strong they may feel, they come and they go.

2 Corinthians 6:14-18 says, "Be ye not unequally yoked together with unbelievers: for what fellowship hath righteousness with unrighteousness? and what communion hath light with darkness? And what concord hath Christ with Belial? Or what part hath he that believeth with an infidel? And what agreement hath the temple of God with idols? for ye are the temple of the living God; as God hath said, I will dwell in them, and walk in them; and I will be their God, and they shall be my people. Wherefore come out from among them, and be ye separate, saith

the Lord, and touch not the unclean thing; and I will receive you, And will be a Father unto you, and ye shall be my sons and daughters, saith the Lord Almighty."

I guess you can see that I made it to that place in the dream where I stopped and turned around while the young men I was running with kept running further and further into the tunnel of darkness. This tunnel of darkness was the mouth of Hell that the Lord God rescued me from. You see, when people become unequally yoked, they are going in two very different directions in life, which made it necessary for me to break away from all of those people. I had to come out from among them. I loved them and cared about them, but none of them could understand nor discern what was spiritually happening in my life. God rescued me from a place in my life that, in my heart, I call Sodom and Gomorrah. I had to flee from that place or die. Much like Lot in the book of Genesis, he loved that great city, it was all he ever knew, but he had to obey and trust the God who created him.

The Bible talks about familiar spirits and God visiting the iniquities of our forefathers and ancestors through many of the generations before us. It has to do with your ancestral bloodline sins, which is the first place the enemy gains his legal right to disrupt your life. What I am really talking about here is generational demons. Where there is un-repented sin, there are legal rights. So, let's say there was a rape or molestation several generations ago that formed a generational curse. Familiar spirits are responsible for these generational curses that crop up in the lives of each generation and cause various sexual sins, so you could imagine that sin may evolve as it gets passed down from generation to generation. Perversion is a stubborn stronghold that is rooted deep into the flesh and down further into the bloodline. Ultimately, the enemy wants to corrupt things in a way that is completely contrary to the way God created it, and ultimately destroy God's covenant with mankind. Perversion is a covenant-breaking spirit. The enemy wants to get us completely twisted away from God's original creation and this is the strategy he uses.

When you look at the condition of our nation, you can see how things continually get worse from generation to generation. Now it is to the point that people are calling evil good and good evil, and we are so blinded and confused in our minds due to the enemy's devices that we can't even identify it until we have a God-moment where God pierces the veil to expose these truths to us. But God says in 2 Chronicles 7:14, "If my people, which are called by my name, shall humble themselves, and pray, and seek my face, and turn from their wicked ways; then will I hear from heaven, and will forgive their sin, and will heal their land."

I didn't know where God was leading me, but knew He was leading me and into pure truth. I sensed there would be yet many new chapters in life to live in a new way, and I learned to appreciate the journey of life no matter what valley I had to go through, no matter what mountain I had to climb. Many nonbelievers would think that this walk with Jesus would be dry and boring, but it is not that way at all. Some Christians might even fall into religiosity, where they are going through the motions and find themselves bored. That's a sign that you may not be seeking out the vision God had for your life and not walking toward your God-given destiny. Maybe you are not bored; maybe you are way too comfortable because you are not being challenged to grow. We were all predestined for something greater, which started in the thoughts of God before He created us. He had a vision for each one of our lives before we were on the earth; much like when you sit down to think about creating something.

Let's say for example, you want to build your dream home. You sit down to think and picture in your mind what you would like for it to look like. You picture in your imagination the color, height, landscape and overall character of the home you would like to achieve. Well that's what God did with each one of us, but we have to tear down everything the world has put on us so we can truly become what He had in mind. But He also gave us a free will to do what we wanted with our life. If you seek God to know what your true purpose is, He will give it to you, but it is up to you to fulfill your calling. I mean, it probably won't just land in your lap or happen by chance, you'll actually have to press in and seek it out. I believe that our purpose for living is to discover our purpose and walk it out in a completely restored fellowship with God. Many people are doing good things, but they are not doing God's things.

"If ye love me, keep my commands."— John 14:15

"Not every one that saith unto to me, Lord, Lord, shall enter into the kingdom of heaven; but he that doeth the will of my Father which is in heaven. Many will say to me in that day, Lord, Lord, have we not prophesied in thy name? and in thy name have cast out devils? and in thy name done many wonderful works? And then will I profess unto them, I never knew you: depart from me, ye that work iniquity."— Matthew 7:21-23

"But you are a chosen generation, a royal priesthood, an holy nation, a peculiar people; that ye should shew forth the praises of him who hath called you out of darkness into his marvelous light. Which in time past were not a people, but are now the people of God: which had not obtained mercy, but now have obtained mercy" — 1 Peter 2:9-10

CHAPTER 8

My Dysfunction Became My Wilderness

After I moved back home, I began to share my testimony with my loved ones of what God had done in my life. God began connecting me to different prophetic voices in the church to speak into my life and began revealing my calling over time, but there were many struggles and barriers that I had to overcome and destroy in order to reach that place of walking in my calling. Being a new Christian was hard for a while, but I was not willing to let go of the truth, and intentionally pressed on seeking God for the inner healing and deliverance that would ultimately transform my entire life. I had to work out my salvation and rediscover myself to become the man God created me to be.

As a new believer, I was excited to discover this new path in life; however, I found myself in the wilderness. I didn't know I was in the wilderness at first; all I knew was that life became harder instead of easier. I found myself in a very dysfunctional state of mind. I really didn't know who I was anymore, so I became deeply depressed and stuck in life. I was desperate for deliverance, but honestly, I wasn't sure if there was deliverance for what I had. When you don't know who you are and no one seems to have the solution to your problem, it is a very difficult place in life to find yourself in. It was very hard for me to see the light at the end of the tunnel of my darkness. But for the first time in my life, I had to start examining and facing my problems. I eventually realized I had to seek God to become the solution that so many have struggled to find.

I had to fight through severe oppression and I had to conquer my emotions. When life seemed to be too overwhelming, I would fall into what I call "shutdown mode." I would become isolated and shut off to the world. I really didn't have real peace in my life. I had an inner peace, yet my thought life was a mess. My life was a big mess. I felt depressed and defeated a lot. I was so consumed by all the things in my life that needed to be restored. When I looked around at my life, all I saw were big messes that I couldn't seem to find the willpower take on. The enemy had attacked every aspect of my life. There were many times I would stay in bed and sleep for days at a time. It was pretty overwhelming coming out of addiction because my finances were jacked up. I was struggling to form a relationship with my daughter and was dealing with a lot of shame and emotional issues. It also took some time for my body to recover from adrenal fatigue that was caused from using meth.

Somehow, I ended up in a very dysfunctional place in life. I struggled to find any kind of balance; everything seemed so out of whack. In my dysfunctional state, I felt lousy and didn't see an end to it. I hated who I was because I really didn't know who I was and especially hated this roller coaster that I found myself on. I couldn't escape to drugs or alcohol anymore, so I escaped to sleep. Ultimately, I felt very stuck. I felt a lot like the Israelites in the book of Exodus where the people said it would have been better for us to stay enslaved in Egypt than to die in the wilderness (Exodus 14:12-15). The wilderness was not easy. It was hard for me. Eventually, I learned to escape into the Lord's presence, and that's where I began to find real peace and strength.

The Lord used this period of my life as enduring trials. 1 Corinthians 10:13 says, "There hath no temptation taken you but such as is common to man: but God is faithful, who will not suffer you to be tempted above that ye are able; but will with the temptation also make a way to escape, that ye may be able to bear it." You begin passing those trials when you embrace the Lord and choosing Him over whatever temptations you are faced with; choosing to press into the presence of God over those sins is the way of escape that He provides. You must find the secret place. You can escape to God through His Word, praying and simply seeking His face. People often think of music when they hear the word worship, but true worship comes from a lifestyle of continually seeking God to know Him. However, music can be part of our worship and helps us enter into intimacy with the Holy Spirit.

God's presence is pure and feels so good compared to the condemnation of those sins of the flesh. Sin is what separates us from God. I learned the way out of temptation, yet I failed over and over again. However, where the presence of the Lord is, there is freedom, and I had a longing just to be in His presence because that's where I found peace and refuge from the many things that plagued my mind. God won't always just set you free, but He will show you how to get free. Sometimes, He won't just heal you, but He will show you how to heal. To find restoration, you have to seek out inner healing and deliverance. The key is to find your stride and yield to His step-by-step guidance through the process. Many times, people want a physical healing or deliverance, but they haven't really gotten close enough with God to hear His directions that would lead to it. Sadly, a lot of people don't really want God, they just want to be healed or they just want the deliverance. He is not a sugar daddy, He's our Heavenly Father that created us, so we should develop intimacy with Him to come to know Him as Abba Father. He is a rewarder to those who diligently seek Him (Hebrews 11:6).

Deliverance is not maintainable without God's increased presence in your life. We can't just visit the secret place, we have to go on in, and make it your dwelling place. Isn't that awesome, God wants you to make His presence your permanent habitation! It took me a long time in the wilderness before I finally reached a point of making that decision permanent in my walk with God. I kept entering God's presence, but I had sin in my life that I was in the process of letting go of and I had a lot of soul wounds.

Eventually, I broke down and told my problems to some brethren, which for me was pretty awkward considering I hadn't opened up about my past gay lifestyle to the men of the ministry. It took a lot of courage and trusting the leading of the Holy Spirit for me to open up to them, but the Lord knew it was time for me to find strength in the brothers. I was scared about opening up and talking about my personal struggles because I feared they would not be able to understand and would reject me. When I reached that breaking point, I learned that I had a lot of walls. It was a relief to realize these men were able to see past my issues and did not reject me. They loved and cared for me even when I couldn't love myself. There was also a prophetic intercessory prayer ministry from a married couple, who are some amazing people of God. They were praying and ministering to my needs. They kept encouraging me to keep pressing on and provided prophetic counsel that brought much needed clarity through difficult times. I do not know where I would be without all of these people, including my Bishop, aligning with the Holy Spirit and operating together as the body of Christ. They looked out for me in prayer so that the Lord's will could be done in my life, and I was able to go a step forward from that point.

I remember standing in my living room and began to notice the spiritual walls that were around me. I literally felt I was in an invisible box, my jail cell, and I desperately wanted out. Those walls became so real to me at that moment. It was as though I could reach out and touch these invisible walls. "God, why am I in this box, and how do I get out?" I was in such anguish, and I felt so lost and confused. I felt like no one could possibly understand what I was going through. God seemed silent. Sometimes it's when He seems silent that He's actually speaking a lot more than we realize because we imagine that we will hear a voice, but there are many ways He will communicate with us. It's up to Him how He chooses to speak to us, not us. Just trust Him every step of the way no matter how difficult it seems at the time. Those seasons won't last forever and they are necessary. Day by day, I could literally feel those walls falling down and could see layers of stuff just falling off in the spirit as a result of the intercessory ministry interceding with fasting and prayer for me. That was my first taste of freedom. Still, I had a lot of wounds that needed to be healed before I would experience complete deliverance, but things were beginning to level out.

The invisible walls came up at such a young age and had been there for so long that I didn't realize they were even there. Like a tattoo or birthmark, you get so used to it that you tend to forget that it's there. I subconsciously erected walls in my life that served as a defense mechanism to protect me from rejection and abuse. Throughout my life, I was afraid that if I let people get too close, they would likely find out some things that might make them uncomfortable, and then I'd have to deal with rejection that way. I didn't realize it, but I was actually rejecting others by keeping people at a distance so that I didn't have to deal with being rejected. I couldn't let go of the past, and I couldn't get past dwelling on the condition I had found myself in so I was in emotional bondage.

One of the brothers, a very devout and honorable man of God gave me these very important words. He said, "You can't do anything about the past, and you may not even be able to do anything about today, but you can do something about tomorrow." That statement helped me to see that I was still holding on to things that did not matter anymore. These things were just stepping stones that led up to this point called the present, and it was time to let go of the past. It was time for me to stop dwelling on the present situations but look up ahead at my future. Why focus on your past if you can't change it? Why sit and sulk over where you are in the present? But look up, look ahead of you and press on towards that vision God has set in front of you. Embrace your future and build that thing! Start speaking the promises of God to your future.

I had to start seeking out the vision God had for my life and then go after it with all my strength. The only way that was going to be possible was that I had to change my thinking. I had to get my thought life under control. My thoughts were so focused on the past and the present that I could not give all of myself to the vision in front of me, which will literally drain the energy from your life. It takes a lot of energy to dwell on things, and it's very unhealthy. If you are focused on what the enemy is doing or has done that is when your energy banks get robbed; but rather, look to the hills from where your help comes. If you are paying attention to everything God is doing, the enemy can't steal your energy and you won't be distracted. I already knew I was going to get my miracle. I didn't know how or when, but my faith knew. As T.D. Jakes would say, "Your knower knows." He is faithful to us even when we are not so faithful. Acknowledge Him in all things and He will make your way straight.

Still, for a long time, I could tell there were still some difficult walls around me. It was like an invisible jail cell that kept me imprisoned so that my true God-given personality could not rise up. Ultimately, it was bondage within more bondage. One day, as I pondered on these walls, I asked God where these walls came from and when they were erected in my life. What was it that happened to me that put these walls in place? That's when He showed me a glimpse in the spirit. I saw myself as a little boy with a male figure standing over me speaking threatening words. Then I was able to identify the walls as the Lord named them to me—shame, fear, rejection, and intimidation were the walls that were built on this event.

This was another confirmation from the Holy Spirit that can be traced back to my early childhood, which indicated an event of sexual abuse where my "jail cell" began. Later on, the Lord spoke to me very clearly in a dream that there was something that started to manifest in my life when I was three years old. After my parents divorced none of the men who came into my life were ever able to show me pure, perfect love, so I grew up with a lot of broken and missing pieces of my soul. For a boy to grow up without a man to look to that can love, guide and care for him with a pure kind of love is devastating to that child's development and identity. It's devastating to the life of anyone to not have a foundation of pure, perfect love in their childhood because nearly all of our struggles in our adult life can be traced back to a place in life that lacked pure, perfect love. Love is always the solution, and every missing piece and broken place of your soul shall be filled and healed by the pure and perfect love of our Abba Father.

The wilderness is a desert place with a mountain. It's very humbling, and it's where things get worked out of us as we are made to examine self very deeply in prayer. It's where the Holy Spirit becomes your companion and in many cases your only friend through the wilderness season; it's about forming a deeper one on one relationship with your Creator, Abba Father. This is where God does a deep work of inner healing and deliverance in our lives that purifies us. This is where God strips away every idol and form of comfort that tends to take His place. It's a process that strips away our fleshly nature and old mindsets, thus breaking away our limitations. It's where we find ourselves in a place of such desperation that we might even want to die, but God commands us to live through it.

We become so desperate for God that we seek Him night and day developing intimacy with the Holy Spirit in spite of the harsh conditions of life. Ultimately, it is where the old you dies off as you go through the dry fiery heat of the desert. The old fleshly nature must die so that your spirit can live. You will identify many demons assigned to your life and will have to learn how to overcome them. At some point, we conquer that mountain and rise above all of life's circumstances as we enter into God's glory. It can be very enduring, but it is for us to seek God so closely that we can hear His every instruction and learn to yield to it every step of the way. In the rest of this book, you will read about the many demons and bondages that I overcame through the leading and revelation of the Holy Spirit in order to be the new creature in Christ that He created me to be. Keep pressing on, there are lots of territory to conquer and giants to kill, but we are headed to the Promised Land!

CHAPTER 9

Restoring the Broken Fellowship with Our Creator

Over the past few years, the Lord kept drawing my attention to the beginning of His word. Time and time again, I kept going back to Adam and Eve in the Garden of Eden. I wanted to see what God's original intentions were for mankind. I began to see that there was something more meaningful and deep to be discovered with God, as I imagined what it must have been like between mankind and God before they ate of the forbidden fruit; before the fall of man. Their fellowship with God was in perfect harmony. God warned them not to eat of the tree of knowledge of good and evil or else they would die (Genesis 3:3-7).

Something happened to them when they disobeyed. As the Lord began to bring more insight to what happened at the fall of man, I realized that mankind didn't die physically, but spiritually. You see, when Adam and Eve ate of the forbidden tree, they were choosing to be their own god by choosing to rely on their own intellect and their own earthly knowledge, rather than walking by the Spirit. It was at that point mankind began walking by the flesh rather than the Spirit. And since then, mankind has been making a mess of things. Nevertheless, here is the perfect love of God towards mankind even after we rejected the One who created us. The Father so loved the world that He gave His only begotten Son Jesus (John 3:16), which was God Himself manifested in the flesh (1 Timothy 3:16), to die and shed His blood on the cross as the perfect holy sacrifice in order to restore what was lost in the garden of Eden, and restore the broken fellowship with His people.

See now, when a person truly gets saved, they have a born-again experience because God breathes that breath of life back into us when we receive the Holy Spirit, which is now possible because of the work that Jesus did on the cross. Without His shed blood, there would be no redemption of sins (Hebrews 9:11-14). Through the Holy Spirit that dwells in us, we have so much potential than most people realize. How is it that so many have the Holy Spirit, but they don't do anything with that presence? After all, having the Holy Spirit is having the mind of Christ according to 1 Corinthians 2:10-16. So let me ask you, what are you doing with your salvation? The Kingdom of God is within you (Luke 17:21). If you are a new creature, are you living to be what He created you to be according to the plan and purpose He has envisioned specifically for your life?

I began to seek God more intimately to restore the fellowship that had been broken by sin; and in the following chapters, you will see the process that the Holy Spirit led me through to break every barrier until the fellowship was restored. I began to seek God's face to walk with Him in the Garden and be restored back to Adam.

"Even now," says the Lord, "Turn and come to Me with all your heart [in genuine repentance], With fasting and weeping and mourning [until every barrier is removed and the broken fellowship is restored]." — Joel 2:12 AMP

CHAPTER 10

Inner Healing; Uncovering the Wounds

My healing began by yielding to the Lord's instruction provided to me through prophetic counsel, as He instructed me to journal about every event that wounded me throughout my life, starting from the very beginning. For most of us, these wounds begin in very early childhood. Rejection can even begin in the womb before birth if, for instance, one or both parents really were not ready to have a child. Also, if the mother has a lot of unresolved issues of rejection, the child can inherit the spirit of rejection. Any type of spirit can be transferred to the child from inside the womb. Often, events such as abuse, rape, molestation, rejection, and abandonment begin to happen to us at such early ages we can't even remember where our problems even began. I started by journaling on each event that I could remember of the things that had afflicted me through life one at a time. Before each session, I always set an atmosphere conducive for healing with anointed music and prayer so that the Holy Spirit is in it with me to bring anything to the surface of my mind that needs to be uncovered. As I wrote in some detail, I uncovered the infected wound and allowed the Holy Spirit to come in and heal that part of my soul. After journaling, I would always soak in that atmosphere during times of healing. It was during these times in my life that I began to feel God's presence so deeply and strongly as He began His deep work in me.

It was hard to grasp how writing could bring healing; and the idea of sitting down and focusing on the hard parts of life was enough to keep me in procrastination. I wasn't doing myself any favors by putting it off. When the Lord gives you instruction and you ignore it or don't pay attention to it, don't expect a lot of other revelation to be released. In other words, you can sit at the foot of that mountain, you can even run laps around it, but you won't conquer it until you've reached the top of it. God always confirms His instruction; in fact, it was confirmed to me that I would find my healing and deliverance as I wrote this book out of faith, and that it would help many other people find theirs as well. Eventually, I got tired of praying for deliverance and healing and nothing happening, so finally I began to yield to the calling on my life. By yielding to the Lord, He began to release the steps one at a time, and as life unfolded, I simply wrote out of obedience. This was the way God chose to work in my life, and once I began writing and fulfilling my purpose, I started to find myself in a process of divine inner healing.

As I started writing in detail about all the wounded places in my life, emotions began to build up on the inside of me as these memories got stirred up. It was like removing the bandage from an infected wound, and allowing the Holy Spirit to come in, cleanse it and heal it. I would write about a certain part of my life, and without holding back, I would just release the emotions that were buried deep inside my soul through crying. As I cried, I released and the Holy Spirit was healing me. As I wrote about each event, I would remember things in more detail. As the memories of these wounds would get stirred up, the Holy Spirit would also be there with me revealing things about those times that hurt and how it had affected me through life.

As I cried, I healed. Depression and oppression began to be released off of me. As I healed, I found that I didn't struggle to get out of bed so much and joy was being restored. I stopped feeling overcome by depression and oppression, and I eventually began to function in life again. I kept coming to road blocks in my walk where I was not growing and the Lord became silent, but the prophetic gifts in the church kept telling me, "Write and you will know what to do next." This was just the beginning stage of my healing, and my desire was to be completely healed and delivered, so that I could prosper in the things that God had intended for.

As I became more and more yielding to the Lord, I began to receive more pieces of revelation to the vision for the calling on my life. Vision is what we all need in order to move forward. If you want to be happy and fulfilled, seek God to reveal your purpose and go after it with all of your strength. If you have a calling on your life and you ignore it, you will never be happy. It's my conviction that every one of us has our own calling designed by God, but each of us must seek it out, discover it and walk it out by faith. That's one reason the prophetic gift in the church is so important because it helps us to find that while we are still learning to hear from God. I never would have made it this far without being connected to prophets and servants of the Lord. Prophets have the anointing to speak into your life to activate you to go forward at very critical times along the way. Prophets are God's chosen vessels that He speaks through to shift, activate, and plant things in our lives; however, every believer should be prophetic to some degree. John 10:27 says, "My sheep hear my voice, and I know them, and they follow me."

John 16:13 says, "Howbeit when he, the Spirit of truth, is come, he will guide you into all truth: for he shall not speak of himself; but whatsoever he shall hear, that shall he speak: and he will shew you things to come."

CHAPTER 11

Unforgiveness

Ephesians 6:12 states, "For we wrestle not against flesh and blood, but against principalities, against powers, against the rulers of the darkness of this world, against spiritual wickedness in high places."

When dealing with unforgiveness, we must understand some things about life. We must understand and accept the fact that people are not perfect since the fall of mankind; we all err in our ways. Only God is perfect, and as His children, we are to reflect what we see Him do. Mankind has a tendency to be influenced by demonic powers operating through the air and from within the subconscious of their minds, which cause strife, bitterness, division, divorce, and all kinds of wicked situations in our lives. This has been the strategy and program of the enemy all along to kill, steal and destroy God's creation. We have all wanted to be forgiven, by the people we ended up hurting somewhere in life after making mistakes that hurt others. Under the darkness, there is always a good, lovable person inside each of us. If we hold onto unforgiveness, God cannot forgive us. Forgiving someone does not mean becoming best friends with the person. It just means, I'm choosing to let go of the hurt so that I can live a happy healthy life. We have to keep our relationships healthy.

Forgiveness is such a big part of our heart. When we finally get tired of being bound by unforgiveness, we can simply find it within ourselves to make a decision to forgive everyone who has ever hurt us. Once we confess these words out loud: 'God, I forgive everyone who has ever hurt me,' what happens is we have just opened the lid of that chamber of our heart that stores all of our bitterness against others along with memories tied to it. Once it has been opened, all of the memories of the things we have been holding onto begin to come up out of the heart and into your mind. This is where most people get hung up, because if we are not discerning "this process," we will end up not letting everything go. But what the Lord wants you to do, as these things start to come up, is simply keep confessing out loud that you forgive them and you forgive yourself in the name of Jesus.

Each time you do this, you will feel those memories and unforgiveness drift further and further away from you. Keep doing this and very soon you will have mastered forgiveness. It has to be a mindset that you will commit to forgiving people for the rest of your life. As a result, your deliverance will come, your heart will be made pure, and you will walk in greater levels of love and peace. Ultimately, you will produce more fruit, your light will be brighter than ever and God will forgive your sins.

CHAPTER 12

Purging the Soul

I dreamed that I was in a small, dim-lit, empty house with hard wood floors and there were some people or friends there with me. There was a closet in the living room, and late at night while everyone was sleeping, I kept going to this empty closet sensing there was an evil spirit in it. I kept going to the closet, opening the door and saying "Jesus Jesus Jesus" over and over to make it leave, but it didn't leave. When I would start speaking "Jesus Jesus Jesus," it would cover my mouth, and suppress my voice so I couldn't speak. I went to the closet multiple times, and then I told the friends that were with me what was going on.

The interpretation: Something hiding deep within the closet of your mind is getting ready to be pushed to surface of your mind, and the devil wants to keep it suppressed. The fact that this evil spirit was left unidentified indicates that Lord is getting ready to expose and identify every demon. The friends that were with me, that I warned about the evil spirit in the closet, represent the confidants God had connected me with. The closet is the sub-conscious and the evil spirit that was invisible or hidden was left unidentified, which means God was getting ready to reveal it by purging them out of the sub-conscious and into the forefront of the mind so that these major strongholds can be accurately identified and then dealt with through fasting and praying the Word. The fact that I visited the closet multiple times to expel the unidentified spirit represents that there was more than one demon bonded together to form one stronger demon within the sub-conscious mind.

Ezekiel 8:7-10 — "And he brought me to the door of the court; and when I looked, behold a hole in the wall. Then said he unto me, Son of man, dig now in the wall: and when I had dug in the wall, behold a door. And he said unto me, go in, and behold the wicked abominations they do here. So, I went in and saw; and behold every form of creeping thing, and abominable beasts, and all the idols of the house of Israel, portrayed upon the wall round about."

Although one may not consider themselves to be in sin, yet the sins of the past still need to be purged because sin leaves fragments of darkness hidden in the pockets of the soul, thereby causing torments and weakness and leaving the soul sick and dysfunctional. We need to identify things that are hidden in the pockets of our soul or hidden in the closets of our conscience; that is the subconscious, which can be very difficult because the enemy keeps himself hidden and then blocks our minds from being able to see and identify it. Demons hinder us from within the sub-conscious part of our mind. Have you ever felt like there was something that was hindering you that has caused you to have dysfunction in certain areas of your life, but you couldn't quite put your finger on it? It is easy to see what is produced on the surface, good and bad fruit, but what is it that is producing dysfunction on the surface; what is under the surface?

When we can identify what's hiding under the surface, that's when we can succeed at doing something about it. We can clean out the closet, but if something is hidden or tucked away somewhere, it will remain there and continue to torment you with emotions and thoughts that do not belong to you. If the enemy put it there, then it's a false emotion, thought pattern, or mindset that doesn't belong to you. Have you ever felt like your mind is too cluttered up to think? Consider how you would function if your sub-conscious was cleared out of all the unnecessary junk from your past. Much like a hard drive on a computer, once in a while, it needs all the junk files cleaned up, and gotten rid of, then it needs to be defragmented. Defragment is what we do to finish the process of cleaning up the hard drive. After clearing all the junk files, what we are left with are good usable files with empty random fragments of empty space between the good files. Defragmenting takes all of the good files and pushes them all together into one organized place and opens up new clear space to work with and store new stuff. Same is with the mind, but we start by identifying all of the junk and deleting it with the blood of Jesus.

What's keeping you bogged down? What's in operation that is causing dysfunction in any given area of your life? Are you ready for reprogramming that will restore your system back to the original blueprint that the Lord intended so that you can truly live out your salvation as a new creature in Christ?

Until we get rid of this stuff, we will keep finding ourselves trapped in never-ending cycles. Setting goals might help, but what I found was that I might achieve a goal or two for a short period but would seem to always find myself right back at square one. I kept wanting to break free from unhealthy cycles but kept finding myself returning to things that were not good for me. Don't become comfortable with any type of bondage. There were certain things that I learned to do sub-consciously to comfort myself through difficult times, such as turning to sin, eating, sleeping too much and isolating myself. I found myself in an endless cycle of bad habits that was wreaking havoc on my health and overall life. I had a hard time getting out of bed because I felt so overwhelmed with life, so I suffered fatigue and became very lax in my life. I procrastinated a lot because I never felt good enough to get anything done. I ate like crap, felt like crap and looked like crap. I let life beat me down and I became lazy and weighed down by a heavy spirit of oppression. It was not an easy period in my life but knew if I kept praying and seeking God that He would pull me through.

Sometimes God won't just deliver you out of a mess, but He will pull you through it. While my wilderness experience was in the form of spiritual oppression, someone else's might be a season of illness that they endure. Either way, it is not meant to harm you, but to call you much closer to the Lord your God to restore you to true worship. Whatever your storm or wilderness may be, will you remain faithful through it? Will you worship the Lord through your storms even when it's not good?

Psalms 34:19 — "Many are the afflictions of the righteous, but the Lord delivers him from them all."

At some point, there comes a time when God says it's time to end all of that in your life if you remain faithful because He loves us and wants better things for us. This wilderness was also like a storm that God allowed to come and tear me down so that He could rebuild me as a new creature in Him. The old fallen fleshly nature had to die so that God could do a new thing in my life. Going through it though, I honestly could not see the end. At some point, it becomes a choice to whether we stay bound or not; at some point, we get so tired of being sick and tired that we build up this determination within ourselves, and we make a decision to press in and take it by force. I mean, if you've found yourself in life this way, are you really going to go down like this or are you going to make a change to impact the world? I say, let's get off our butts, plunder the gates of Hell, and save our families.

Let's make an impact in a lost and dying world and set the captives free! It is not always easy to break free from cycles, systems and programs that have been put in place, but life can truly be so much better than the devil ever wants you to know. If a person truly wants to be free, then they will be, but unfortunately not every believer truly wants to be free. They will go on and on about how troubled they are, yet they never put any effort into their deliverance. It takes a lot of energy for any believer to be in bondage because our spirit is always at war with these things. It is not over, so be encouraged and inspired. If you have found yourself stuck, it's most likely because God has called you forward, so be strengthened and encouraged by the unveiling of truth that comes forth in your life.

The enemy just likes to keep our minds bogged down so that we can't move forward, but once we break free, we will become a lot more effective in the Kingdom. We've been called to be effective and productive in the Kingdom, and you can be effective every single day—not just some days, but every day. If you feel drained of energy and never seem to feel rested, it could be because the devil has been keeping your mind busy and tied up with a lot of emotions, negative thinking, and worrying. The devil speaks lies through our subconscious feeding our mind thoughts of negativity to make us feel hopeless so that we never move forward. If we are not discerning these thoughts, or voices correctly, we end up speaking what we hear in our minds. Life and death are in the power of the tongue, and it's what comes out of the mouth that defiles us. We can speak blessings or we can speak curses. It is not over; there is a Way!

Once you get cleaned up and purged of everything, that's when you can move on to the next level. But if nothing changes in you, then not much will change around you in your life. I believe I wrote this book for some amazing people who want to move forward but have been stuck. I wrote this book for people who are desperate for transformation in their lives but haven't found the keys to unlock the rusty old lock that has been seemingly stuck forever. I also wrote this book for those of us who have even gotten lost in the process, but this book will help you get back in the race and finish what you may have started some time ago. Just keep abiding in the shadow of the Almighty because He loves us so much He won't just leave us where we are. He will set us free and take us to our destinies. God won't change you all at once. It is a process, so just find your footing and let God order your steps. Everyone's healing and deliverance seems to be different because there are so many different combinations of bondages, but this book was written to reveal a strategy to help God's people see and understand that there is a process and that there is an end to it; there is a light at the end of the tunnel.

There is greatness in all of us. Don't get frustrated and don't get a bad attitude because a bad attitude will keep you stuck. Keep humbling yourself through the process; seek God with all your heart and you will make it. It's not even that far away, but the devil likes to make you think you'll never make it. In those times of frustration, I just began to ask God for wisdom, knowledge, and understanding; to change my mind and my heart to reflect His, through being transformed by the renewing of my mind. It takes a lot more energy to hold on to that bad attitude and frustration, but renewing our minds restores our energy. Frustration is simply a sign that we have a lack of wisdom of some kind. Keep the word of patience for once it is a little while, then you will receive the promise.

Hebrews 10:36 says, "For ye have need of patience, that, after ye have done the will of God, ye might receive the promise."

He changes us little by little, bit by bit. He wants us to always have some sort of need because that is what keeps us seeking Him, and He is always pursuing you and has been for a long time whether we realize it or not. I'm sure if you were to sit down and journal about your life, you can see the footprints of Jesus in the sand. You cannot take your past with you to your destiny so you've gotta let it go. He wants to make you whole. And what can make you whole again? It's nothing but the Blood of Jesus.

Sometimes God will ask you to do something that won't make sense to anyone. It won't make sense to the analytical mind. The Lord ordered my steps one time to be a car salesman at a dealership. When the opportunity opened up and God confirmed it, I knew I was going somewhere to be challenged to grow and hoped that God would prosper me there. God took care of me there, but it was only for a season. I was probably the most introverted person ever hired there, but someone saw my potential. I soon realized that God didn't necessarily send me there to sell cars, but to break me out of my shell a little bit. I got used to speaking to people, finding and leading them through a process of finding what they wanted and doing my best to sell it to them. But it was very challenging as an introvert because introverts don't particularly like chit chat and small talk.

You've got to be able to work the customer a little bit and put on a different face. I had a hard time finding things in common with most people. A lot of the things that people seem so interested by, I simply don't find all that entertaining or important. But this was my battleground where I began to be challenged to question things as to why it was such a challenge for me. I had to examine things deeper to find out what was wrong with me that made this situation so difficult and challenging to me while it seemed so easy and natural for others.

To the untrained eye, this wouldn't make sense, but for me, I was there to begin being purged, which led to identifying my actual strongholds. I soon realized I was not there to sell cars, but to identify my demons and destroy those on a battleground in the spirit. What I thought was going to be my launching pad ended up being my battleground where God was forcing me to deal with my issues. It was time to find out what was causing so much turmoil, confusion and dysfunction in my life. Like in Ezekiel's vision, I had to dig through the wall, open the hidden door to the sub-conscious to look inside to see the sources of all my problems. In the next chapters, God exposed all of the demons that were rooted in the rooms and closets of my soul and brought me through to my deliverance. The soul is the temple of the Holy Spirit and He is jealous of what we allow to inhabit His space.

"For if the blood of bulls and of goats, and the ashes of an heifer sprinkling the unclean, sanctifieth to the purifying of the flesh: How much more shall the blood of Christ, who through the eternal Spirit offered himself without spot to God, purge your conscience from dead works to serve the living God?" — Heb 9:13-14

"Moreover he sprinkled with blood both the tabernacle, and all the vessels of the ministry. And almost all things are by the law purged with blood; and without shedding of blood is no remission." —Heb 9:21-22

Every branch in me that beareth not fruit he taketh away: and every branch that beareth fruit, he purgeth it, that it may bring forth more fruit. — John 15:2

CHAPTER 13

Fear

The first thing I saw in operation was fear. It's crazy to imagine how I could have lived such a wild life so fearlessly, yet I had so many internalized fears that I never paid attention to. You could be dealing with fear and not even know it. I suppose we could say I was in denial about it to some degree. Since I was never able to see any real solution to my problems, it was easier to block this from my mind. But at last, I found the solution to my lifelong issues as the Lord showed me how to untangle and break the yokes to all of them. God places the best things in life on the other side of fear. I have seen some people struggle with tapping into faith because they fear the unknown or fear that they might put too much energy into something, but faith is the evidence of things unseen, so have faith to have faith in something. That mustard seed would not be there without a purpose!

Every seed has a purpose; to be planted and to produce something (think about it.)

Look at what happened to Peter when he stepped out of the boat and onto the water with Jesus. Peter stood on the water for a moment, but fear overtook him so he began to panic and sink into the water. Although fear caused his faith to fail him, it was our Lord Jesus who saw his faith and His outreached hand pulled Peter back up to safety. God won't allow you to perish in something he has given you faith for. So remember, even if your faith fails you, God will reach down and catch you if you are taking that big step of faith. He's waiting for that step of faith in your life. It is okay to let go and trust God. If faith is the evidence of things unseen yet you fear the unknown, how will you walk by faith? Overcome fear by the word of God. I've even had witches come to destroy me along the way and even had demons come to attack me in my sleep during times of breakthrough, but God has always covered me.

Once I began to identify major strongholds in my life, I began to examine things further to understand how these were manifesting through the sub-conscious into my life holding me in bondage so that I could not go forward. I came out of the world yet it still had its hold on me. I began to notice how certain behaviors that I always had were manifested through fear. I never would have identified some of these things as forms of fear if the Lord had not made it surface in my mind to reveal it to me. As you are being purged, the things that are hidden in the sub-conscious will begin to be pushed to the forefront of the mind. That is when we can identify the roots and foundations to our personal issues, and when we can identify it, that is when we can begin to deal with it in the spirit.

I began to really pay attention to my behaviors throughout each day and reflecting on how they were in the past. It was clear that I was extremely uncomfortable in certain settings, such as meetings, and if I was ever put on the spot where I became the focus in a group setting, I would even feel embarrassed. I was extremely self-conscious, struggled with social anxiety, had a tendency to be passive, and lived with a pattern of becoming withdrawn and isolating myself from others at different times throughout my life. The Holy Spirit began to make these things stand out in my mind so that I could deal with it.

Once we can identify it, we can begin to come out of agreement with it. After examining and gathering information, I was able to tie all of these sub-conscious behaviors to one thing, which was fear. Fear was the first major stronghold that the Lord revealed to me, but then I had to find out where fear came from and how it got there, which I wrote about in the next chapter. The enemy had me wearing myself out trying to overcome the many different behaviors that were being produced on the surface. The key is to go beneath the surface of your problems to identify the actual strongholds and then deal with them at the roots through praying God's word and fasting. This kind only comes out through praying and fasting just as Jesus told the disciples in Matthew 17:21.

The word of God says in Mark 3:27, "No man can enter into a strong man's house, and spoil his goods, except he will first bind the strongman; and then he will spoil his house." Jesus also gave us specific instructions on prayer in Matthew 6:16 and in that, He said, "when you fast" not "if you fast." God also instructs us to take up the whole armor of God and in Ephesians 6:17, scripture refers to "the sword of the Spirit, which is the word of God."

Isaiah 55:11 says, "So shall my word be that goeth forth out of my mouth: it shall not return unto me void, but it shall accomplish that which I please, and it shall prosper in the thing whereto I sent it."

God's word will not return void, so get equipped and get prepared. Simple prayers work for some things, but if you want to uproot and destroy the works of darkness in your life, you are going to have to get serious, and use the weapon that God has given you. Study the Word and pray the Word.

After identifying this stronghold, I began to renounce and bind fear anytime I was entering into one of those uncomfortable settings. At times, I could feel the level of anxiety drop, and I was able to feel more comfortable in meetings; other times, not so much. Obviously, this was just the beginning. Sometimes it just takes a revelation from God to gain an understanding of what we are really dealing with in order for things to initially begin to break off. But in cases like mine, it will require fasting and praying to completely uproot these issues.

I also observed how fear manifests differently in other individuals. While fear seemed to make me very introverted, fear can also cause a person to be very manipulative and controlling out of a sense of insecurity. Manipulation and control are forms of witchcraft and are signs that a person needs deliverance from the spirit of Jezebel. A person can easily identify the negative emotions that are produced on the surface, but we have to learn to get revelation from God to expose what is hidden.

I had a lot of internalized fears that were formed in the subconscious. I also found that as the stronghold of fear was beginning to break down, that the Lord was pushing me out onto the water a bit further by challenging me to start up prayer in church services and prayer circles in order to make me overcome the fear of speaking in front of people. These are things that have made me feel like hyperventilating. At first, I did not understand why the idea of speaking in front of a large group of people would make me feel that way, but as I looked within myself, I realized that I was deeply afraid of what people thought about me or how I looked, which makes it impossible to speak to an audience while that type of fear is manifesting. I would even avoid it, as I was scared to death that I would embarrass myself. Can you say extremely self-conscious! Fear causes us to over think things to the point of not being able to do what we should be doing; fear has a lot of excuses and causes procrastination. Fear is a liar and will make a liar out of you because fear causes people to lie. Fear is a lying spirit.

There were a lot of these fears that developed at such a young age that I never knew I was operating in fear. I always wanted to be a social butterfly, but I just couldn't. I would typically find crowds and conversations at times to be rather draining. I will probably always be an introverted person as I believe it is part of my God-given personality. Introverts can be very bold when they need to be once the spirit of fear is broken. Introverts tend to be very deep thinkers, authors, and visionaries. They often have great ideas, but struggle with confidence. The devil just wanted to keep me from speaking because he knew I was called to speak the truth to many people. If you are a person who struggles with fear, know that you are called to be very bold and you have a voice. Whatever you struggle with, you are the exact opposite of that in the spirit. After the Lord revealed fear, the next stronghold that surfaced was rejection.

CHAPTER 14

Rejection and Fear Go Hand in Hand

Again, coming out of the sub-conscious rejection was something that I never identified within myself until the Holy Spirit pushed it to the forefront of my mind through the process of being purged. I always felt that I was different from other people. I carried a feeling deep inside myself of feeling unwanted. I never felt like I belonged, and I had a very low self-esteem. But at the same time, I never paid enough attention to how I felt, so I never identified any of my problems. I erected many walls and boundaries that served as a defense mechanism, which kept people pushed away and at a distance. I figured that if I could keep people out, they wouldn't be able to identify some things in me that might make them uncomfortable. I feared that people would be disgusted with me about things that I didn't know how to change so it was a way of subconsciously avoiding more rejection. I began to reject myself and carried feelings of low self-worth from an age too young to remember, possibly even from the womb. I hated who I was and the way that I perceived myself. Deep within myself, I felt that I was so different that I couldn't be loved or accepted so on a very subconscious level; I rejected myself which produced self-hate. I couldn't easily give love to others, nor could I very easily receive love. This made me a very selfish person who, up to salvation, was only out to satisfy self. I suppose you could conclude that all of the destructive things I did in life were subconscious-misguided efforts to love myself.

In a perfect world, each one of us would have been raised with a foundation of pure and perfect love in every aspect of our childhood. When I talk about rejection, in essence, rejection is just the absence of love and acceptance; mankind's inability to love with pure and perfect love-outside of God. The absence of a father figure in today's society plays a very critical role in today's generation, which stunts the growth and development of our character and identity. I call this "arrested development." Sadly, this pattern seems to get passed down generation to generation. The solution is, turn to the Lord with your whole heart in repentance to be restored to the One who created us.

Rejection, the absence of love, tends to be something that we all deal with because we are not living in a perfect world due to our fallen nature. Children need to have the natural affection from both parents in order to be balanced; otherwise, they can grow up starving for that missing affection and can become sexually confused, especially if they've fallen victim to any single event of sexual abuse. It leaves an empty void that often gets filled with spirits of lust, ungodly relationships, and addictions. It tends to lead to a life of destructive behaviors and rebellion. I also never recognized how important that missing link could be until I started living my life for the Lord. As the Lord led me down paths of righteousness and truth, He began to reveal all of the things that factored into my "bondage."

Our souls need the love and affection from both parents in order to grow up balanced. When a soul grows up without the love of either parent, or perhaps without both parents, it leaves a big empty void in that person's life and they go through life subconsciously cramming things in, in an effort to make themselves feel fulfilled and whole, but we are never made whole by these things. I can reflect back on my life and see that I used drugs, alcohol, sex and unhealthy ungodly relationships to fill the emptiness in my life. These all served as false comforters, and lust is a false sense of love. Lust combined with our emotions produces intense feelings that many people confuse with love, but this type of "love" is worldly and it will never last. This is why you see so many people in and out of relationships and if they get married, it ends in divorce because so many people are driven by lust rather than the Holy Spirit.

As I began to examine my emotions and behaviors for rejection, I noticed that I had a strong sense of feeling unwanted and felt very inadequate around other people, which would cause me to withdraw and isolate myself. I was more comfortable with my life of solitude than I was around a lot of other people, even my own family. It's hard to feel that acceptance when you feel that people couldn't possibly understand. I just felt so different from other people.

The mind has a crazy way of navigating our thoughts around certain things in order to avoid ever having to look at it. I didn't want to see that I didn't feel accepted because that meant I would have to feel rejected. No one wants to ever feel rejected. Although the Lord revealed fear first, fear is actually rooted in rejection, and in the same context, rejection births fears. For example, because I was wounded by rejection, I had a fear of rejection, fear of embarrassment, fear of failure, feelings of inadequacy, social anxiety, etc. and became a more introverted, timid type of person. I had to realize that is not who I am because that is not what God created me to be. I believe my condition was the result of a generational curse, which caused me to be born into a situation that would end in divorce, which in turn would cause me to grow up in an environment with no real male role model to hinder my growth and development as a man because of the calling on my life. In other words, it was a demonic program issued by Satan to destroy my identity. My condition was the result of the iniquitous sins of my ancestors to the third and forth generations of my ancestral bloodline. Rejection can be a generational demon that crops up in the lives of many wreaking havoc on God's people. This begins the process of twisting the minds of people into something that was not intended by the Creator. Rejection opens the door for spirits of fear, perversion, shame, self-rejection, worthlessness, poverty, confusion, as well as many other spirits; rejection is known as the door keeper.

"Behold, I was shapen in iniquity; and in sin did my mother conceive me. Behold, thou desirest truth in the inward parts: and in the hidden part thou shalt make me to know wisdom." — Psalms 51:5-6

"The Lord is longsuffering, and of great mercy, forgiving iniquity and transgression, and by no means clearing the guilty, visiting the iniquity of the fathers upon the children unto the third and fourth generation." —Numbers 14:18

Just a short time before my total deliverance, the Lord gave me this dream. I was in a house and through the windows into the backyard, I saw two giant beasts playing together. One was a horse, and the other was something hairy like a wildebeest. They were gigantic and my mother reached her hand out of the window of her house to pet the horse and wanted to keep them. I said to her, "Mom, if you keep those things, they will destroy your house." "What are they?" I asked. She replied, "They travel from place to place looking for a place to stay, and together they complete one another."

From this dream, I concluded that the Lord was preparing me for deliverance and was revealing that the spirit of rejection and the spirit of fear travel together, and together they are complete. I mentioned that the Lord was preparing me for deliverance because what the Lord said in this dream reflects Luke 11:24-26, "When the unclean spirit is gone out of a man, he walketh through dry places, seeking rest; and finding none, he saith, I will return unto my house whence I came out. And when he cometh, he findeth it swept and garnished. Then goeth he, and taketh to him seven other spirits more wicked than himself; and they enter in, and dwell there: and the last state of that man is worse than the first."

I needed to get myself in order by getting the sin out of my life; I had to get my flesh under control. God was calling me higher, and my set time for deliverance was drawing nigh. At last, soon I would be delivered from the prison cell that kept me bound my whole life. However, deliverance does not come without spiritual resistance.

CHAPTER 15

Slaying the Dragon: Pressing in to Win

Don't get lost in the process! For me, the process that God has taken me through, was like a mountain that I had to climb. There was no way around it. After fasting for this thing and then that thing and then another thing, I grew weary and I let things distract me from my assignment. And because at that vantage point, I could not see an end to the process, I stopped. I got to a point where I just didn't feel like I could go on another fast, so I figured I would take a little time to recalibrate. But little did I know that the constricting spirit of delay had shown up in my life to stop me from getting the rest of my deliverance. That little bit of time turned into several months. During that period, I found that my life became very boring and frustrating. The Lord was telling me to finish, but I was struggling along. The spirit of delay comes upon you when you are moving forward. It wraps itself around you like a python, squeezes the spiritual life out of you and ultimately paralyzes its victim so that you cannot move. Leviathan is depicted as a water serpent dragon, so he has an elongated body that can wrap around a person to constrict them. Then the Lord began to speak to me very clearly through a dream followed by a prophet.

I dreamed that a friend of mine went to this minister about me and the minister said, "This is what I've known about Matt for a long time now — he never presses in to win." Upon waking up that morning, meditating and praying about the dream, I was like dang I never press in. But it didn't take long for it to occur to me that the Lord was simply saying to press in. So over the next few days from that dream, it was all I could think about as the Lord had planted this seed in me to press in, and it was beginning to sprout and soon to take root.

I regularly attend the 5 o'clock prayer service held each Sunday evening at my church, and after prayer, I walked up to the exact same minister that was in my dream. I asked him to pray over me, specifically asking him to "anoint my press in." I never told him the dream as it was never actually necessary. The funny thing was that he didn't pray over me. He spoke a word from the Lord over me, which is even better because the prophetic word activated me. He said, "The very moment you realized that you have to press in, therein lays your total victory." He said, "Do you know what I mean by that?" "Kind of, but not exactly," I replied. He said, "So many people only make it so far, and they stop because they never realize that they just need to press in." This is why I love going to a prophetic church because I can't imagine trying to find my way through without these gifts empowering me and operating in my life. We all need some help from time to time, and it helps a lot when you are able to get a word that will activate and confirm what God has already allowed you to discern. We need that so that we are not just aimlessly going after things. We need specific direction.

It took me some time to figure out exactly how God wanted me to press in and exactly what that might look like specifically for me at that particular time. For me, I began finding my footing by eliminating any distractions, so I disabled my Facebook account, cut out YouTube and ate light in the evening so that I could focus. I fasted—fasted—a couple meals through the week, and committed more time to prayer each night, which brought me back into alignment with God and my God-given assignments. I found my sense of direction as I tuned in to the Holy Spirit. The Lord began to show me fresh revelations as to what my next step would be. The Lord had previously revealed to me two main strongholds, which were rejection and fear, but this time He was revealing the actual strongman in charge of these strongholds; the spirit of Leviathan. As my discernment in the matter increased, I began to hear and see what the Lord was communicating to me; as well as bringing things back to my memory, such as dreams and hidden messages He had previously given me.

I dreamed that there was a very tall muscular man that was chasing after me. Somehow, I wrestled this huge man down to the ground, and with a rock double the size of my hand, I hit him in the head over and over until his head was crushed and he was seemingly dead. I picked this man up, dragged him over to the edge of a steep hill and hurled him over it. I walked away fearfully thinking to myself, I hope he is dead because if he's not, he is going to kill me.

This was to let me know that this would be a self-deliverance much like David and Goliath. David destroyed the giant Goliath with a stone, which was done by the power of the Lord. This story can be interpreted as a picture of self-deliverance. 1 Samuel 17:49-51 says, "And David put his hand in his bag, and took thence a stone, and slang it, and smote the Philistine in his forehead, that the stone sunk into his forehead; and he fell upon his face to the earth. So David prevailed over the Philistine with a sling and with a stone, and smote the philistine, and slew him; but there was no sword in the hand of David. Therefore David ran, and stood upon the Philistine, and took his sword, and drew it out of the sheath thereof, and slew him, and cutoff his head therewith. And when the Philistines saw their champion was dead, they fled."

In another dream, there were aquatic eels in my house and populated around the property. These had a head that resembled the anaconda snake with many big hooked teeth; its body like an eel was approximately three feet in length with the pattern of a python. Upon waking, I was under serious demonic attack, which a prophetic intercessor confirmed at that time it was caused by Leviathan. I woke up feeling very emotional and confused.

Leviathan causes emotional and mental bondage causing all kinds of confusion as it twists and pulls on the thoughts and emotions of its victim. This is a mind-binding and mind-bending spirit. He can show up in dreams as the crocodile or alligator. Much like either of these creatures, he hides camouflaged under the surface of the waters near his victim and at just the right moment when you let your guard down he leashes his attack upon you pulling under the water to drown you twisting you around and around to cause great confusion and weakness, and ultimately death. As it is in the natural, it is in the spiritual.

The Lord gave me a dream with several scenes. The first scene was a prophet who being very pregnant. As she positioned herself on the floor of the sanctuary, going into labor, she said, "this is coming forth now!" One of the other scenes was in a college ministry classroom setting. The class had not started yet so there were a few students who had arrived early and were talking and getting acquainted. The lady on the front row said, "Hi. I'm just here visiting. I'm Catholic." Another lady sitting a few rows behind her said with a quick stern voice, "Oh, we don't believe that way!" When she said that the atmosphere became tense, but then another woman spoke from the other side of the classroom and said, "No she's right. His name was George and it was in Luke chapter 4."

The name George is not mentioned in Luke, but in my research I found that Saint George was a Tribune in the Imperial guard who struggled with a fire breathing dragon and was said to be of the highest rank as well as a protector of the people. The story of George depicts a dragon that the entire village was at the mercy of this fire breathing dragon. Saint George slayed the dragon and saved the village. From then on Saint George was known as the deliverer of the captive. In other stories written, Saint George was known to cultivate and prepare the soil as he tears up the stony ground; prepares the hearts of believers so that when seeds are planted they will produce a fruitful harvest. He was martyred in year 303 because he refused to renounce his Christian faith and would not submit to pagan beliefs.

Luke 4:31-35 talks about a man possessed of unclean spirits, which cried out, "Let us alone!" Jesus rebuked the demon saying, "Hold thy peace and come out of him." After being thrown down in the midst of them, the demons came out of the man and he was instantly delivered. If you read that passage of scripture carefully, you will see that it says Jesus rebuked the demon, which is singular, but prior to that, the demon cried out "let us alone" indicating more than one demon. However, these demonic spirits were bonded together inside the man to form one stronger demon. The same was true for me.

In Luke chapter 4 you also see Jesus being led into the wilderness being tempted by the devil for forty days and then preaching the acceptable year of the Lord and the beginning of his healing and deliverance ministry. I believe this prophetic dream reveals the birthing of the healing deliverance ministry, the high calling God has placed on my life to be a deliverer of the captives, a protector of the people, and to prepare the hearts of believers.

Luke 4:18-19 says, "The Spirit of the Lord is upon me, because he hath anointed me to preach the gospel to the poor; he hath sent me to heal the brokenhearted, to preach deliverance to the captives, and recovering of the sight to the blind, to set at liberty them that are bruised, To preach the acceptable year of the Lord."

Over the past few years, I had been under serious spiritual oppression to the point that in a lot of ways, I felt paralyzed not having the strength or motivation to function on a regular basis. I had experienced some degree of oppression most of my life, but more so during my previous years as a new born-again Christian. I had never felt so oppressed in my life as I did as a born-again Christian. It was all caused by these demonic spirits that were assigned to attack my life and to hinder my growth.

After gathering all of my information from the Holy Spirit and from the Word, I was ready to "press in" and slay the dragon. During my time of delay, the Lord was equipping me with the sword of the Spirit. That is how we defeat our enemies—we apply the word of God. I know from reading the book of Job that Leviathan is not a devil that you want to put your hand on so it was not something I took lightly upon myself. The Lord showed me in the dream where I crushed his head that if you get him, you'd better kill him.

So how did I do it you ask? I didn't, the Lord Mighty in battle did it for me. I participated through prayer and fasting to release the arm of the Lord and crush the heads of Leviathan (Psalms 74:14) shattering my oppressors into pieces, strip off the scales of pride (Job 41:15), release the sword of the Lord to slay the dragon and cut me loose from an evil inheritance (Isaiah 27:1); taking up the whole armor of God and doing all that I can do to stand, I stand therefore covered under the blood of Jesus (Eph 6:11). I proclaim that because I have set my love upon the Lord, He has delivered me out of all of my troubles (Psalms 91:14). Because I put all my trust in Him, He encompasses me as a shield (Psalms 5:12). No evil shall befall me, no plague shall come nigh my dwelling and angels have been given charge over me (Psalms 91:10-12). I sought the presence of the Lord and the anointing that breaks every yoke (Isaiah 10:27). I bind rejection, fear, and perversion (Matthew 18:18). I loose the spirit of burning to burn up everything that is not of God (Isaiah 4:4). I loose agape love because perfect love casts out all fear (1 John 4:18). I repair the everlasting doors and ancient gates and open them to the Lord God Almighty inviting Him in to be mighty in battle on my behalf (Psalms 24). I fasted for three days, prayed these scriptures and dared not to break this fast until it was complete.

A week or so following the fast, I sensed and anticipated my breakthrough, which came during our church conference. The conference lasted four days and I being called to serve in the church, was there serving each night. Each day from that fast, I began praying in powerful tongues more intensely to the point of travailing in the spirit (Romans 8:26). Each night of the conference, God's presence seemed to become stronger and stronger upon me and within me as I began to feel fuller and fuller of God's presence. I was filled up and overflowing with the Holy Spirit. It was the anointing and being in that anointed atmosphere after fasting that I needed. It was the anointing that broke every yoke of bondage and it was powerful.

One night of that conference, as I walked into the church, immediately the Lord directed me to a prophetess who spoke over me. She said she was proud of me because now the devil was behind me and ministered to me about Paul and Silas was thrown into a prison cell and they prayed and praised aloud to the Lord at midnight. The Lord shook the foundations of the prison. She said "It was the foundations that had to be broken in order for the prison cell to break open, because when the foundations are destroyed, the house cannot stand." It was when she spoke this word over me that our sovereign Lord both confirmed and finished this work in my life to set me free from my prison cell of fear and rejection that I had been in my entire life.

"And when they had laid many stripes upon them, they cast them into prison, charging the jailor to keep them safely: Who, having received such a charge, thrust them into the inner prison, and made their feet fast in the stocks. And at midnight Paul and Silas prayed, and sang praises unto God: and the prisoners heard them. And suddenly there was a great earthquake, so that the foundations of the prison were shaken: and immediately all the doors were opened, and every ones bands were loosed." — Acts 23:-26

The last day of that conference, we had daytime sessions for leaders. I attended and a pastor asked me to play a part in his presentation. I was never one to be comfortable being center of attention in front of a large group of people, but when I did it, I didn't feel uncomfortable or embarrassed. I found that I was comfortable and actually having a lot of fun with it. That was when I knew God had definitely done something and I felt so free. I had never felt so free and liberated in my entire life up to that point.

However, there were still a couple more demons that I had to get delivered from in order for my deliverance to be complete. This was my mountaintop experience. Finally, I was no longer in the wilderness, but I made it to the top of my mountain. I knew at that point the rest of my journey was going to be a lot quicker and easier going back down the other side. Be careful to guard the gates of your soul with all your strength. If you let the devil entice you into sin, you will be opening the doors of your soul allowing the devil back in to destroy your soul. I was yet on my way to the Promised Land!

CHAPTER 16

Guarding the Gates

"Keep thy heart with all diligence; for out of it are the issues of life." — Proverbs 4:23

The attack that comes right after your breakthrough to reverse your deliverance, will come in the form of whatever you were delivered from. Since this deliverance was for rejection, the attack came in the form of rejection. The wisdom that I acquired for this is that rejection indeed is the door keeper for fear, self-rejection, depression, suicide, perversion and many other unclean spirits.

It's important for us to be in powerfully anointed churches where the Lord's presence and power can flow, otherwise how will we experience deliverance? You may not be able to find a ministry that conducts an exorcism type of deliverance per say, but you should be able to find a ministry where anointed men and women of God have enough discernment and spiritual authority to help you drive the devil out of your life. It's not God's will for His people to be left in bondage. Deliverance and healing is our right. Deliverance is the children's bread, but it is your responsibility to learn how to stay delivered.

Rejection manifests in the gate of your emotions, which is your heart. If the heart is left unguarded, rejection can manifest emotional turmoil, and when a person feels unloved or rejected, they will often subconsciously find ways to escape those feelings such as sin or other false comforters. If a person falls back into sin after deliverance, it's just like the word says, a spirit will return to its home with seven spirits greater than itself. If that happens, it can be a very difficult situation to find yourself in, and you will need the help of a deliverance ministry.

"When the unclean spirit is gone out of a man, he walketh through dry places, seeking rest; and finding none, he saith, I will return unto my house whence I came out. And when he cometh, he findeth it swept and garnished. Then goeth he, and taketh to him seven other spirits more wicked than himself; and they enter in, and dwell there: and the last state of that man is worse than the first." — Luke 11:24-26

My pastor preached that we have to be able to pull our emotions out of our situations and just speak the Word. Guard the gate of your emotions with the chest plate of righteousness. Master your emotions or else your emotions will master you. Often times we end up acting out of our emotions and wind up saying things that we later have to apologize for. My Bishop preached, 'Your emotions will take you on a trip, and are an entry way for the enemy,' which certainly is true. We can all examine our lives and identify times at which we allowed our emotions to take over, making things worse than they already were. I thank God for my Bishop because it is such a blessing to come to the house of God and receive such wisdom and clarity from the Lord through him. We need that in our lives and it is vital for our Christian walk; otherwise, we would become stagnant or get lost along the way. I could not be where I am today without being planted in such an anointed ministry. That's why God said in His word that He would appoint to us pastors because He knew upon being saved, we would need direction from someone who could hear from God in ways that we can't (Romans 10:14; Jeremiah 3:15). It's not that we can't hear from God, but it is the order and system put in place by God Himself.

We have to be careful not to let our emotions and imagination lead us astray. God does not speak to us through our emotions. While He may speak to us through the realm of our imagination at times, we have to be very careful that our imaginations are not being influenced by our emotions or by demons. If something doesn't feel quite right in your spirit, pay attention to that. I had a prophet tell me, "It's when what you feel in your spirit matches what's in your mind, that's what you go with." Sometimes God is telling us, but we fail to hear correctly because we allow our emotions and imagination to lead us too much. Spirits can influence our emotions, thoughts and imaginations so be careful that you are not being led by the wrong spirit. The only time that God speaks to people through emotions is when the emotions manifest through the gift of discerning of spirits, which is different from this topic.

CHAPTER 17

Marine Spirits

And he put forth the form of an hand and took me by a lock of mine head; and the spirit lifted me up between the earth and the heaven and brought me in the visions of God to Jerusalem, to the door of the inner gate that looketh toward the north; where was the seat of the image of jealousy, which provoketh to jealousy. And behold, the glory of the God of Israel was there, according the vision that I saw in the plain. Then said he unto me, Son of man, lift up thine eyes now the way toward the north. So, I lifted up mine eyes the way toward the north and behold northward at the gate of the altar this image of jealousy in the entry." —Ezekiel 8:3-5

For thou shalt worship no other god: for the Lord whose name is Jealous, is a jealous God. ---Exodus 34:14

Then said he unto me, The iniquity of the house of Israel and Judah is exceeding great, and the land is full of blood, and the city full of perverseness: for they say, The Lord hath forsaken the earth, and the Lord seeth not. ---Ezekiel 9:9

And he spake unto the man clothed with linen, and said, Go in between the wheels, even under the cherub, and fill thine hand with coals of fire from between the cherubims, and scatter them over the city. And he went in in thy sight. Now the cherubims stood on the right side of the house, when the man went in; and the cloud filled the inner court. Then the glory of the Lord went up from the cherub, and stood over the threshold of the house; and the house was filled with the cloud, and the court was full of the brightness of the Lord's glory. ---Ezekiel 10:2-4

Jesus answered them, Verily, verily, I say unto you, Whosoever committeth sin is the servant of sin. ---John 8:34

Sexual sin can be one of the toughest barriers to dismantle, especially when we've been in bondage to it our whole life, but we must have an understanding of exactly what we are dealing with in order to come out of agreement with it. When we acknowledge it as sin, we repent, and by acquiring wisdom and understanding, we come out of agreement to experience freedom. In my experience, I began to identify some things, such as sexual encounters and drug use in my dreams. Many of God's people are in spiritual bondage to this perverse demon that causes defiling dreams. I don't remember ever having dreams about using drugs until after God delivered me from the addictions, which was the devil's desperate attempt to tempt me into my old lifestyle, but the temptation to drugs was completely gone at this point. I believe the forces of darkness can manipulate the dream realm from inside our souls to keep people in a state of confusion, depression, hopelessness, etc, so it is important for us in our efforts to be pure to purge these areas.

As the Lord allowed, I began to discern that the people in my dreams were actually a manifestation of a Succubus marine spirit. These types of dreams are demonic strategies to form soul ties to the victim through the dream realm, which is why the demon behind perversion can be identified as a "spiritual spouse." It is a spirit that forms a soul tie with its victim, and people are usually completely oblivious to this in their lives until the Holy Spirit starts revealing it to them, however they are quite common. Typically, these spirits will keep the same image, but it's not uncommon for them to change their identity in these dreams. Many of these dreams are manifesting during levels of sleep where one could not remember the dreams, other times they can be quite vivid and this demon operates in the dream realm to keep the victim's mind programmed for sexual sin and sexual confusion. You cannot experience true deliverance from sexual confusion if you are still experiencing it in your sleep.

The spirit spouse is often passed down through a generational curse and enters the person's life through any event of molestation, rape, or incest; and it can even be transferred from a sex partner, or it can even be put on you through witchcraft. Basically, any type of sexual sin gives this demon permission to invade your life, including masturbation and pornography. These are unclean spirits of perversion, which come to molest and rape you in your sleep. They plant lustful images in your mind while you sleep and keep the sexual nature of their victim aroused so that they are driven away by their own lust during wakeful hours. They also manifest through the imagination in daydreaming and pollute your thought life. These spirits are relentless and can seem impossible to break free from.

You may not even be able to remember these dreams and unclean sexual acts that are being performed on you in your sleep, but this is how the enemy plants its seeds, through the subconscious, to cause sin to manifest in your life in order to stay rooted and to maintain its hold on you; to keep you tangled up in bondage, addicted to sex, masturbation, porn and the like. Ultimately, this is a covenant-breaking spirit in the sense that it causes you to have intense uncontrollable urges to commit sins that separate you from the Lord's presence, and to stop you from ever becoming the man or woman God created you to be.

"Then said he unto me, Son of man, hast thou seen what the ancients of the house of Israel do in the dark, every man in the chambers of his imagery? For they say the Lord seeth us not; the Lord hath forsaken the earth." ---Ezekiel 8:12

All of this is a desperate attempt to keep you in bondage to stop you from taking off and being effective in ministry; ultimately, to keep you separated from God and to hinder you from ever having a totally restored covenant with God. The double-minded man is unstable in all his ways. It keeps you "looking in the rearview mirror" causing you to reflect back on your old lifestyle and can even get you to consider going back to it to escape all of the false emotions of torment it produces in your life. False emotions are emotions that demons cause to manifest in you. These emotions that you deal with are often produced or birthed from demonic strongholds. If you have not gone through deliverance, you do not know who you truly are, because your mind has been under the influence of demons probably since early childhood or even from birth. Quite often, generational spirits of perversion will crop up in early childhood in an unseemly event that opens the door to bring in lust, torment and confusion. The devil is a liar and has no good intentions for you. Satan is out to kill, steal and destroy you, your marriage and your seed, but God came to give you life and life more abundantly. This devil does not look anything like the image it takes on in your dreams. It is a gross horrific monster that ultimately wants to lure you and your children into the pits of hell, so that it can torture your eternal soul with ongoing pain and sorrow. Demons feed off of your sin, pain and negative emotions. Some powerfully anointed deliverance ministers believe that demons are the disembodied spirits of the Nephilim and they have made their home inside many of us with one plan in mind; to live out their evil fallen nature through mankind. The sins we commit, along with any torment and misery they cause is what they thrive on.

If you are dealing with this, know that you are not alone, and many men, women and children are dealing with the same thing, but are too ashamed or embarrassed to admit this to anyone, therefore it can be difficult to find true deliverance from this demon. But now that God is giving you this revelation, you can begin to identify these manifestations in your life, you can begin overcoming it. Declare divorce and renounce it—it has no right to claim you once you've received salvation. You belong to the Lord God and He is jealous for His people. You are His bride and temple, and you should not allow any darkness to remain in you; for you are a new creature in Christ, behold all things become new.

Paul said in Ephesians 5:3 says, "But fornication, and all uncleanness, or covetousness, let it not be once named among you, as becometh saints."

Any time you commit any type of sexual sin, you are continuing to stay in agreement with this spirit and that is what fuels it, leaving you feeling oppressed and drained of energy. This demon is stubborn, relentless, and desperate in its attacks to keep you entangled in sin. Once God revealed the monster that had been hiding in the closet, I was able to begin disciplining myself and crucifying the flesh to overcome it. Fasting and resisting are how we crucify our flesh and purify our souls creating a clean and holy place for the Holy Spirit to dwell in; as you pray that your old fallen nature to die off. As a Christian, fasting should be included in your life regularly. However, don't do it religiously, but spiritually by the leading of the Holy Spirit.

If you struggle with lustful looks on other people, masturbation, premarital sex, looking at nude images, addiction to porn or anything that causes that feeling of lust to rise up, you are giving this spirit more power over you; but as you crucify the flesh and bind them, demons get weaker and weaker. Remember your eyes are the windows or gates to the soul so if you entertain lust with your eyes, darkness will fill your temple. And yes, masturbation alone is a common sin that opens the door wide open for spirits of perversion, shame, embarrassment, hopelessness, condemnation, guilt, fantasy, daydreaming, torment, depression and suicide. It is a very stubborn spirit, but you can overcome it.

These spirits are responsible for many divorces and broken homes. The order of God in the household is God first, then the husband, then the wife. The problem is that many families are not submitted to God, and even if they are, if this spirit is present in the man or the wife, it causes problems in the marriage that often result in divorce. If they have children, this becomes a broken home. Anytime the order of God in the household is broken, children end up raised in a broken-home situation. They also cause sleep disorders similar to sleep apnea. It will sit on the chest to suffocate the victim and cause sleep paralysis. Unclean spirits can cause sickness and disease, as well as wreak havoc on our relationships. If these are invading your life, you must get free in order to have a healthy marriage. Seek help from a local deliverance ministry and prophetic intercessors to help pray and guide you through this.

You have to have a lifestyle of reading and studying God's word. Being filled with the Holy Ghost and praying in unknown tongues will empower and build you up to overcome all bondages. This is because He knows better what to pray to effectively destroy any barriers that have been set up in your life. Romans 8:26 says, "Likewise the Spirit also helpeth our infirmities: for we know not what we should pray for as we ought: but the Spirit itself maketh intercession for us with groanings which cannot be uttered." When you are walking in the Spirit, the enemy doesn't have power over you, but the slightest sin leaves a crack for these demons to creep back in and pull you back into the flesh leaving you tired and weak. If you've been saved, then you are called to walk in the Spirit, and since you've been called to walk in the Spirit, sin can make you feel quite miserable.

However, we tend to keep going back to it because it is all we have ever known. The more you enter into God's presence, the easier it gets to overcome these things. You are on a journey of rediscovering your identity, which can only be found by learning to stay in His presence. You will find that it is true that everything you will ever need or want can be found in Him. In order to overcome this demon, you will have to press in and take your relationship with the Lord to a much deeper level. You have to find it within yourself to seek the Lord with all your heart and all your strength intentionally and relentlessly to know Him.

At the root of perversion is the addiction to it so you have to break the addiction and the mindset. This too, can be done through fasting and praying. You must get to a place in life where you have decided upon embracing purity in order to trade the works of the flesh for God to be your dwelling place. In all truth, these demonic spirits are assigned to our lives to keep us separated from God's presence, and to hinder us from having a restored fellowship with our Creator; we have to return to the Garden of Eden. We must be restored back to Adam before the fall of man, after all, that is the reason Jesus came to pay our ransom, set the captives free and to fill us with His presence to restore what was lost in the Garden of Eden at the fall of mankind.

The days of relying on our own intellect should be over at this point. As believers, we should find ourselves completely reliant on the Holy Spirit for every move in our lives. We have to have a real relationship with Him. After all, that is exactly what we were created for; to worship Him in spirit and in truth. There is a deeper chamber of His heart that, too often, is left undiscovered. Too many people today are lukewarm and have no clue what it is like to be filled with and immersed in the presence of God. We should be pressing into this blessing with all of our heart in fasting and prayer to be filled and refilled so that our lamps are always full and ready for the Lord (Matthew 25:1-13).

Even when Jesus rebuked the Pharisees when they questioned Him about fasting, He said, as written in Mark 2:19-21, "Can the wedding guest fast while the bridegroom is with them? As long as they have the bridegroom with them, they cannot fast. The days will come when the bridegroom will be taken away from them, and then they will fast in that day." That is to say, we are supposed to fast for His presence as we seek Him, and then in verse 22, "And no one puts new wine into old wineskins. If he does, the wine will burst the skins- and the wine is destroyed, and so are the skins. But new wine is for fresh wineskins." That is to say, we fast to crucify the flesh and to be filled with His Spirit. It is for His presence to fill us, and then for us to also be in His presence; Him in us and us in Him. That is a picture of the baptism of the Holy Ghost.

If you struggle with homosexuality, know that it is in you to be attracted to the opposite sex. This type of spirit of perversion suppresses the God-given natural attraction and influences same-sex attraction. This has been Satan's plan against mankind all along. He hates God, hates God's people, and wants nothing more than to twist our minds in the opposite direction of God's original creation and separate us from our Creator. Once a person goes through the process of removing every elemental factor and behavior of sexual sin and confusion (images, porn, masturbation, lust of the eyes and the demon of perversion) and once the demon behind all of this is cast out by commanding it to go and not to return in Jesus' name, we close every open door: the sexuality, eyes, emotions, self-will, dream realm, imagination, and even memories. We then bind every gate keeper. Once all of these elements have been removed and steps have been properly taken, a person will naturally revert back to the way God designed him to be; he will revert back to his natural instincts—restored back to Adam.

James 4:7 says, "Submit yourselves to God. Resist the devil and he will flee from you."

Luke 11:34 says, "The light of the body is the eye: therefore when thine eye is single, thy whole body also is full of light; but when thine eye is evil, thy whole body is also full of darkness."

Every time you resist the temptation to sin, your resisting is not in vain. Your resisting is what purifies you, and in turn, you are becoming more and more filled with God's light; that is the Holy Spirit. Remain in the vine by staying in God's word. Discipline yourself to read God's word every single day even if its less than a chapter for this is where you will gain the spiritual strength to walk by the Spirit and resist sin. Spending time with the Lord at the start of each day will also empower you, even more, to walk by the Spirit. If you do these things, I promise you will feel the Lord's strength and His presence so strongly throughout each day. Who knows what rewards He might manifest for you.

In order to get free and maintain your deliverance, your love for God has to grow. You have to fall in love with God's presence and go after God every single day and you have to have a relationship with God's word. It's got to become your reason for living. You have to get to a place where you love God enough to choose Him over this sin in your life, which only comes by spending time in His presence. I have heard other men of God tell me, "God's presence is even better than sex." The more you seek Him, the more you will hunger and thirst after Him. Be intentional as He is intentional and spend time alone with Him. He must be first in your life. Just to be completely honest, if you are not giving Him the first part of each day and truly seeking Him with all of your heart and strength, then you have not yet made Him first. In other words, He is still somewhere in the background or sidelines of your life, but as you inch closer and closer to Him, the broken fellowship with God is being restored.

There were times along the way that I had to be honest in examining myself to see that I wasn't able to love God in a way that was pleasing to Him, that I needed to love Him a lot more, but the solution was as simple as admitting it and letting God know I wanted more. He will give you anything you ask for. In order to be delivered, my faith also had to grow and as you relentlessly go after God and spend time in His presence, your faith will grow. After all, how will you have faith to believe God can and will deliver you if you still don't really know Him. I am willing to be honest, I still feel that I don't know Him enough; I still want more. I crave more so I am always seeking for more. I have spent enough time in God's presence that if I drift away from the secret place, I am quite uncomfortable and on edge. You must find the secret place and make that your dwelling place. Don't just visit it but go on in and live there.

There is something very powerful about being up seeking His face during the second and third watch of the night. Jesus was always going to spend time with the Father during these times. When we think about prayer, we often think of asking for things or petitioning, but it is also about sitting in the Lord's presence and just listening for His instructions and then yielding yourself to Him. There are things He is speaking specifically to you that you cannot hear from where you are; some things can only be heard from inside the deepest chambers of His heart. He is welcoming you into this place of intimacy, but it is up to you to press your way into it. Surely, there is more to this watered-down Christianity than what people are living, but all we have to do is tap into it. That's where we are transformed. In His presence, there is freedom because whatever demons that may be attacking you cannot stand in His presence. Demons lose power in the presence of God, for every knee shall bow to the Lord Jesus Christ.

Sometimes we mess up a lot along the way, but the Lord is faithful to pick us back up and deliver us out of our troubles so long as we repent. Sometimes the key to true repentance is to ask the Lord to put our hearts in a position of true repentance so that we can put an end to habitual sin and get back in the race. Don't allow yourself to get comfortable being in bondage. The Word says humble yourself and He will lift you up. If a person truly wants to be delivered, they will be. There is a powerful anointing that comes with exercising the gift of tongues: it can drive the demons out of you.

Matthew 3:11-12 says, "he shall baptize you with the Holy Ghost, and with fire: Whose fan is in his hand, and he will thoroughly pure his floor, and gather his wheat into the garner; but he will burn up the chaff with unquenchable fire."

So, for example, if you got delivered, but the demon got back in through an open door, the Holy Ghost can and will push that thing back out as many times as it takes until you're able to maintain your deliverance so long as you are seeking it. But the key ingredient is faith, which can be increased through fasting. Faith also increases as we build ourselves up on our most holy faith, praying in the Holy Ghost according to Jude 1:20-21.

When we fast, it crucifies our flesh and empowers us to walk in the Spirit. Let me just inform you: Your flesh does not believe in God! You might probably have to fast several times to get your flesh under control. You want your fleshly "fallen nature" to die off so that your spirit can live. In Mark 9, when the disciples could not cast the demon out, Jesus rebuked them for their unbelief. The disciple then asked Jesus to help his unbelief. Jesus cast the spirit out, and then in verse 29, He gave them instruction saying, this kind only comes out by prayer and fasting. Fasting is what helps us deal with our unbelief. If we are in need of something to happen in our lives, but don't seem to have the faith to obtain the promise, we can fast and increase our faith. We must have a greater level of faith to cast demons out and to heal the sick. When you go after it, you have to know without a doubt that it is coming out in the name of Jesus. And by faith, you can command it to "go and enter no more." Too bad, so sad, devil! However, if you keep feeding a stray dog, it is going to stick around.

I dreamed that there were aquatic eel creatures in my house. These eels had the head and many hooked teeth like that of an anaconda, fins of an eel, three feet long, and the scale pattern of a python. In the dream, I was finding them in my house and tossing them out the door into the front yard. Then I went outside into the yard to find a dog dead with the tail of one of these creatures hanging from its mouth, and there were many of these creatures all around the property.

This interpretation of this dream refers to Proverbs 26:11 — "As a dog returneth to his vomit, so a fool returneth to his folly." When we go back to sin, it is like returning to your own vomit and consuming it, which brings forth spiritual death. Aquatic eels represent the marine spirit of Succubus. The fact that there were so many populated around the property could possibly mean that there was a demonic portal of perversion open somewhere, or it is possible that these were being sent through powers of witchcraft. There were a few other dreams where the Lord revealed that I was being attacked by witchcraft, and it is typical that Satan will have witches assigned to God's people to stop them from walking out their true purpose and callings. Do not be ignorant of Satan's devices.

I remember a time where the devil had me so pulled back into sin that I wasn't sure I would be able to make it back to God. I was in such a dark place, but I eventually got around to making myself pray to the Lord to bring me back to him and to put my heart back into a position of repentance. It wasn't easy for me to speak those words because I had backslid far enough that the enemy had my mind so twisted around that I was rationalizing trying to think of ways to exit the church and considering my old ways. It was hard to pray that prayer because I knew what I had done was intentional, and with all of the thoughts I let go through my mind, I knew I didn't deserve forgiveness. But God answered because it is not His will for any of us to perish. Deep inside, I truly wanted the Lord to rescue me from the entanglement. I said, "God, how can you forgive me after the evil thoughts I had?" He responded with, "It's a small thing for Me," and then He gave me this song called 'Narrow Road' by Rick Pino. The lyrics that spoke to me that day I will never forget: "You say the wide gate looks so beautiful but destruction is its end."

Matthew 7:13-14 KJV says, "Enter ye in at the strait gate: for wide is the gate, and broad is the way that leadeth to destruction, and many there be which go in thereat: Because strait is the gate, and narrow is the way, which leadeth unto life, and few there be that find it."

What I found out, though, is that sin and that way of life felt so generic compared to the pure tangible presence of the Lord. After consistently being in the presence of the Lord, I simply couldn't let myself choose that sin anymore because I grew to love His presence more than the sin. I love God and I love being able to be in His presence, and you cannot have both because sexual sin quenches God's spirit from your soul. When you commit sexual sin, a demon like the spirit of python wraps around you and squeezes God's spirit out of you, and you begin to die spiritually.

When you sin you bring spiritual warfare upon yourself. That's why God said in Job 41:8, "Lay thine hand upon him, remember the battle, do no more." Because when we commit these sins, it is like laying your hand upon the dragon. And you cannot handle the dragon. This demon likes to keep people in a back and forth motion in their spiritual walk, in and out of bondage to wear you out and ultimately cause you to give up. There is victory when we press in and run towards our callings.

The Lord's instruction for the temple: Ezekiel 44:1-4, "Then he brought me back the way of the gate of the outward sanctuary which looketh toward the east; and it was shut. Then said the Lord unto me; This gate shall be shut, it shall not be opened, and no man shall enter in by it; because the Lord, the God of Israel, hath entered in by it, therefore it shall be shut. It is for the prince; the prince, he shall sit in it to eat bread before the Lord; he shall enter by the way of the porch of gate, and shall go out by the way of the same. Then brought he me the way of the north gate before the house: and I looked, and, behold, the glory of the Lord filled the house of the Lord: and I fell upon my face."

Your soul is the Lord's temple, and as the royal priest, you have strict instructions to guard the gates so that nothing else enters it. Once you have overcome all bondages and have become a sealed vessel, it is your God-given responsibility to protect the glory of God that has been placed within you with the authority and power He has given you. Take heed, that no man take your crown. Revelation 3:11-12 says, "Behold, I come quickly: hold that fast which thou hast, that no man take thy crown. Him that overcometh will I make a pillar in the temple of my God, and he shall go no more out: and I will write upon him the name of my God, and the name of the city of my God, which is new Jerusalem, which cometh down out of heaven from my God: and I will write upon him my new name."

CHAPTER 18

Ahab Programming; Arrested Development

For some reason, the most obvious demons tend to be the hardest to identify within yourself. They are most obvious to mature Christians, who know and understand the spiritual realm, by which their discernment has been exercised by the Holy Spirit. I honestly thought I had named all of my personal demons by this point, but as I sat before the Lord in the wee hours of the morning, He began to reveal the spirit of Ahab. At last, all of the dots connected. Finally, it made sense why I seemed to always have various relationship issues, and up to this point, had never been able to fully walk out my manhood. But the Lord, who is able to do exceedingly abundantly more than we could ever ask for, because I have set my love upon Him, has delivered me out of ALL of my troubles. And you, my friend, are next!

Ahab is the male that has been emasculated by various afflictions in life stemming from early childhood. Probably, he was passed down from your ancestral lineage. He is not effeminate but does not act like a real man. Men who are effeminate are probably under the spiritual influence of Jezebel. The spirit of Ahab can be in women also but is most commonly in men. Jezebel is most commonly in women but can certainly be in men too. These spirits do not care about gender. Ahab is a leader but tends to be a weak leader; if he is married, he tends to be a weak husband and father figure, while Jezebel keeps him beat down. He does not take his position in the household to properly lead his family.

According to the order and design of our Creator, men are commanded to lead the household. It's God first, then the husband, then the wife; but instead, his Jezebel wife begins to take on the man's leadership role in the household. He can be very submissive, which makes him a great church leader in that respect, but is very passive in nature, which makes him weak. Ahab feels inferior and avoids conflict at all cost. He could be known as the peace keeper and will even take the blame for things in order to maintain peace. He never defends himself, he is a people pleaser, channels anger and frustration internally, feels sorry for himself, becomes depressed and emotionally unstable over his feelings of inadequacy, and loathes self. He can be lazy, careless and irresponsible as a result of self-hate since he doesn't love himself enough to take charge of his life. He tends to be self-centered, tends to be timid and cowardly, he can be introverted and uses masturbation, porn and other addictions to escape how he feels internally. He can be all talk, but when confronted face to face, he will try to smooth it over. He doesn't necessarily take control and lead because of his lack of confidence in himself, so he looks to others to lead and guide him because he feels inadequate at that level. He is afraid of the responsibility that comes with leading a group, and therefore often becomes Jezebel's enabler.

I call it Ahab programming because in all truth parts of our personalities are shaped by rejection and fear, therefore I don't believe that many of the people we call Jezebel or Ahab are actually demonized by those spirits. These are simply people in the process of becoming who God created them to be as they come out of agreement with the lies the enemy formed about them within their souls.

Jezebel seeks out such people, whether in a leadership role or not, to control and manipulate. Without an Ahab present, Jezebel cannot operate at her fullest capacity. People with the Jezebel spirit will be drawn to people who have the passive Ahab spirit. Jezebels always want to find people who they can dominate and control, which explains why I seemed to get connected with people with a possessive nature. In the world, I was always in relationships with people who were controlling and manipulative. Even people who were strictly in the friend zone would always somehow lure me into their sphere of influence; or webbing if you will. Jezebels are only interested in Ahab because, in some way, Ahab will enable them to meet their hidden motives and agenda even if it is to calm a sense of insecurity within herself. If you are an Ahab, know that you are called to be an Elijah and the only reason these Jezebels have been in your life is to keep you beat down, pushed down and to keep you in a mode of Ahab programming. If you have some Jezebel friends, I don't care how long you've been friends, tell them to get lost and don't look back. The Ahab spirit in you will try to play guilt tricks on you to make you second guess yourself. Trust me; that feeling of guilt is not the Lord's. It is not God's will for us to be in unhealthy relationships. You can love these people from a distance. It's your time to transform!

As a born-again Christian, through general discernment, I found that I would resist such people, but if I ever made the mistake of making friends with one, the Lord would always intervene because it would be an unhealthy alliance. If you are fully submitted and yielded to the Lord, He will take care of you because He has plans to take you places in life that you have never been before. I would find that I had an uncomfortable gut feeling in my spirit about certain people that would cause me to put a wall up, but I didn't understand what I was discerning at the time. It was the Lord protecting me, but at the same time, I became more withdrawn because there were so many of them. At times, I would think well it's just me and maybe I need to learn to love people more. Well, it seems that way to an Ahab because the Jezebels will always find him. Ahab is like a magnet for Jezebels. People with Jezebel spirit do not know they have it most of the time. Jezebel has a tendency to hide out until the person under her influence forms a connection, and then she will begin to slowly but surely sink her claws in.

At first, your conversations can seem very enriching, and you will think it is a good alignment until you find yourself entangled in her web, which is weaved by her pet spider who weaves a web of deception around your life. Jezebel is very, very, common, and there are different types of Jezebels. Some are very obvious and rebellious, and others are like the girl who never grew up and seems so innocent. She can seem very innocent and harmless, but she has hidden motives and agendas that she will never admit to. She has a tendency to become defensive easily. She might even keep you tied up in a meaningless conversation where she goes on and on about herself just to drain you of your energy. I call them drainers because they will always somehow corner you and drain your energy with their conversations that have no real point and no end. Ridiculous! In the church, she is very religious and goes after leadership roles, and when she spots an Ahab being elevated, she will try to befriend him.

On the other hand, Ahab is the exact opposite, which is why in many marriages you will see an Ahab married to a Jezebel. Or in other words, a very calm passive person is married to a control freak. Rejection and fear can make a person very introverted and passive, which is the Ahab; or it can make the person very outwardly controlling and manipulative, which is Jezebel. According to some deliverance ministries, you will not normally see a person who has both Ahab and Jezebel operating through them, while other deliverance ministries disagree. I would think this would be a higher degree of schizophrenia as these demonic personalities take turns controlling the victim. People who have been severely afflicted by rejection and abuse can become schizophrenic. Most people have some degree of schizophrenia, but normally at such a low level, that it is very undetectable. I suppose someone with regular mood swings might qualify as a low level of schizophrenia, but until a person goes through deliverance, they will not know what the true roots of their problems are.

In severe cases, such as mine, people will not know their true personality, nor what they are capable of achieving until they have reached total deliverance. My condition was severe because of the call of God on my life. That is why Satan did everything in his power to take my mind and personality and twist it into the exact opposite of what God created me to be. Whatever your struggles are, know you are called to be the exact opposite in the Spirit. I struggled with so much internalized fear because I am called to be very bold and powerful in the Lord's Kingdom; where I used to represent perversion, I now represent purity. Every weakness I had, the Lord turned into strengths.

2 Corinthians 5:17 says, "Therefore if any man be in Christ, he is a new creature: old things are passed away; behold, all things are become new."

The Lord revealed the structure of what my bondage looked like. Basically, there was the spirit of Ahab, who opens the door to perversion; the Succubus spirit; then there was the spirit of Leviathan, who was the ruling spirit of the spirits of rejection and fear. There were several minions under all of these stronger demons, such as depression, suicide, hopelessness, passivity, self-pity, and worthlessness; all of which, were bonded together, and rooted in self-rejection—the murdering spirit of self-hate. I call it a murdering spirit because it murders its victim's personality and identity in Christ. But as you can see, the Lord started at the bottom to remove the foundation, which was rejection and fear. Then we took out Succubus and Ahab. Again, I tell you, we do not know who we truly are as new creatures in Christ until we have gone through deliverance. I believe God put such a degree of desperation in my life to be free so that I would press my way through and reveal keys and strategies to help other believers walk out deliverance. To God be the glory of my life and yours!

To overcome the spirit of Ahab, yyou need to get filled with the anointing of Jehu. That is the anointing of the Holy Spirit used in deliverance ministry. Press in and become what God created you to be; a powerful Tribune for God's Kingdom, a deliverer of the captive. Anointed warriors of God such as David, Elijah, and Jehu, that is who you were created to be like. And as you go through inner healing, you are being made whole and becoming the man or woman God intended for you to be.

2 Kings 9:1-9 says, "And Elisha the prophet called one of the children of the prophets, and said unto him, Gird up thy loins, and take this box of oil in thine hand, and go to Ramoth-gilead: And when thou comest thither, look out there Jehu the son of Jehoshaphat the son of Nimshi, and go in, and make him arise up from among his brethren, and carry him to an inner chamber; Then take the box of oil, and pour it on his head, and say Thus saith the Lord, I have anointed thee king over Israel. Then open the door, and flee, and tarry not. So the young man, even the young man the prophet, went to Ramoth-gilead. And when he

came, behold, the captains of the host were sitting; and he said, I have an errand to thee, O captain. And he arose, and went into the house; and he poured the oil on his head, and said unto him, Thus saith the Lord God of Isreal, I have anointed thee kin over the people of the Lord, even over Israel. And thou shalt smite the house of Ahab thy master, that I may avenge the blood of my servants the prophets, and the blood of all the servants of the Lord, at the hand of Jezebel. For the whole house of Ahab shall perish: and I will cut off from Ahab him that pissseth against the wall, and him that is shut up and left in Israel: And I will make the house of Ahab like the house of Jeroboam the son of Nebat, and like the house of Baasha the son of Ahijah:"

Elijah is what you are created to be like, but Satan has been robbing you of this calling by turning you into an Ahab. Command open the ancient gates and everlasting doors only to the King of glory, the Lord strong and mighty in battle to come in and fill you with His presence, healing and restorative power, according to Psalms 24. Renounce Ahab and all other spirits by naming them out loud and telling them that you want no part of them by speaking boldly in the authority of Jesus Christ. In the same manner, bind each strongman by identification in the name of Jesus.

Demonic spirits suppress your God-given personality, abilities, giftings and anointing, so if you bind anything, always command it to loose the very things they have been suppressing from your life, such as your true personality, masculinity and manhood, sexuality, joy, soundness of mind, boldness, gifts of the Spirit and anointing in Jesus' name. Also, anytime you bind something, you should always loose the opposite to counteract the demonic power, for example when you bind fear, loose boldness and perfect love. Perfect love casts out all fear. Another example would be to bind perversion, and loose purity and righteousness. Command it to "go and not return, in Jesus' name." Lastly, close every door to the emotions, will, sexuality, dream realm, and any other door you can identify, and seal every door shut with the blood of Jesus.

Reprogramming comes by spending time with Abba Father and seeking His face in the wee hours of the morning. As in any deliverance, you must have enough faith to do it, which only comes by spending time with the Lord in His awesome presence. You can fast all you want, but no deliverance is maintainable if you are not immersing yourself in His presence. You must also be committed to studying His Word daily; otherwise, you will not be strong enough spiritually to get free. I strongly recommend getting baptized in the Holy Ghost and with fire, as this will empower you to overcome each demon in your life, as well as empower you with the operation of ministering gifts listed in 1 Corinthians 12:7-11.

Paul said it best in 1 Corinthians 12:31 KJV, "But covet earnestly the best gifts: and yet shew I unto you a more excellent way." Remember, it is your fleshly nature that doesn't have faith, but your God-given spirit absolutely does. So, if you get yourself crucified through fasting, you will automatically start having greater levels of faith. Praying in tongues, fasting and saturating yourself in God's presence is what builds your faith up to be able to cast the demons out, and gives you strength through the process to keep going. Without this gift, I promise you, I do not know how I could have gone through so much self-deliverance. Most of all, you must seek God's presence continually. You have to go after God with all that is in you.

I had a very difficult deliverance. One hindrance I had was that I didn't know how to let go of the very things that kept me bound. It was all I ever knew much like Lot, who sat in the gate of Sodom and Gomorrah. God was commanding him to leave that part of his life behind to start over with something new that Lot had never done before. Like Lot, I had to trust God to give me something better than I had ever had. And finally, my other major hindrance was that I was seeking my deliverance more than I was seeking Him. We can become so focused on our deliverance or, in other cases, healing that we are only seeking for those things; then they become idols, when in all truth we should be seeking His face more than these things.

I found myself seeking after my deliverance so much that I couldn't get delivered. If you seek His face, you will always get His hand. It is about a restored fellowship with God, and if you will just seek Him with all of your heart just to know Him that's when your deliverance and healing will manifest. He has to be first in your life every day. I have grown to learn to get before the Lord to seek His presence at the beginning of every day no matter what time I have to wake up; doing this will increase His presence in your life and enable and empower you to walk by the Spirit instead of the flesh. As a result, your life becomes fruitful dramatically. Prayer is not just you petitioning God. It should be just as much about listening to hear His instruction. In fact, if you get this right, you will find that you won't have to petition God so much.

Deliverance ministry is rare, and when there isn't one available, sometimes you have to press in to become your own deliverance minister. Binding is a method used to get the demon into a weakened state making it easier to cast out. At some point, you have to get connected with real deliverance-minded people who are not afraid to cast out demons. Binding a demon and casting it down does help the person feel free, but it's usually a temporary fix because the demon will always crop back up eventually, and then the person has to keep going through the motions. That's very unhealthy for the individual and makes their journey of deliverance quite difficult and frustrating. If you are someone who is in a church that does not do deliverance in casting out demons, I encourage you to first pray and let the Lord lead you, and then find a reputable deliverance ministry that can help you. It is in His presence that we become transformed into what He created us to be.

You become a brand new creature day by day as you go through the process of allowing the Lord to peel back the layers of all the stuff that didn't belong to you, all the fear, rejection, abuse, pain, trauma, confusion, etc...As he peels back all of the layers, He is unwrapping you as a gift because you are a gift to the body of Christ. You are a gift to God's people. The wrapping may not have been so pretty, but what is inside is what truly counts, what's inside is the most valuable part about you. You see, Satan and his forces of darkness of this world have planned to keep you hidden from this world by placing layers upon layers of things upon you to hide who you truly are because he's afraid of you. He's afraid of what you could do to his kingdom if you ever became who Creator God created you to be.

Proverbs 6:31 says, "But if he be found, he shall restore sevenfold; he shall give all the substance of his house." Once the thief has been caught, he has to repay sevenfold. Everything the devil has stolen from you; he has to pay it back to completion according to Gods word. Everything that you could have, would have, should have had will be repaid: your finances, your career, your identity, your personality, your ministry, health etc...whatever it was that the devil has been robbing you of, he has to pay it back — the recompense of the Lord. Now, forward into the promised land.

PRAYER OF SALVATION

Have you just finished reading this book and you are yet to give your life to Jesus Christ? You need the love of God first—you need to become born again by accepting Jesus Christ as your personal Lord and Savior. That's the first step to true deliverance—freedom from Satan, sin, and sickness. When you become born again by accepting the Word of God, then His Holy Spirit will become a seal upon you, thus making you God's inheritance, a child of God. And from there, He will begin to show jealousy upon you when the enemy rises against you.

I encourage you to take that bold step today, regardless of what your family and friends may say about you when you go tell them about this "new creature" experience. You have your own life to live, and a purpose to fulfill.

Please, pray a prayer of faith for your salvation:

Dear Heavenly Father,

Lord, I believe that you died on the cross for my sins. Romans 10:9 says, "Because, if you confess with your mouth that Jesus is Lord and believe in your heart that God raised him from the dead, you will be saved. "I make you Lord and Savior of my life. Lord, I desire to have a relationship with you. Lord, I confess any sins of _____. I repent Lord. Wash me in your blood in Jesus' name Amen.

About The Author

Matthew Whitaker is a regular small-town guy from southeast Missouri, who ha s experienced life outside the bubble. He is a first-time author of a God inspired book, which is the first of many books, and prophetic intercessor. He is a future evangelist who has the heart of a servant and the heart of a warrior. Matthew stands on the front line for God's people. Through the many struggles in life, He has grown to have such a heart for the lost and the wounded.

His passion is to lead people to Christ, set the Captives free, and help God's people discover their calling and purpose so that they can reach their destiny. He is a glory carrier and his ministry goes beyond the church walls into the streets, market places, to reach into the trenches to pull the lost to safety in a lost and dying world! .

It is his desire that through writing and ministering that he will stir the hearts of many people to discover something deeper and more meaningful; that he will inspire and provoke people to discover God in a way that goes beyond their initial salvation, but that people would be inspired to live a life of true worship and find themselves leading a lifestyle of discovering God every day for the rest of their lives. It is Matthew's prayer that this book provokes people to seek God to restore the fellowship with our Creator and release an unveiling of the mysteries and secrets of deliverance of God into the lives of many so that God's Kingdom advances and prospers in the earth.

INDEX

A

addiction, 46, 123

B

battle, 108, 140

believers, , 107

blood, 82, 89, 145

bloodline, 57

C

confusion, 8, 31, 106

D

deliverance, 63, 78, 101, 112–13, 128, 139, 141–43, 147

devils, 59, 108, 129

Dysfunction, 60

E

evil, 23, 57

F

forgive, 78–79

forgiveness, 78, 130

G

gates, 112, 121, 130, 132

God, 1–3, 46–49, 51–53, 56–59, 61–66, 70–72, 76–77, 91, 93, 108–9, 116–17, 122–30, 139, 141–44, 146–47

J

jealousy, 116

Jezebel, 94, 134–37, 140

K

knowledge, 71, 86

L

lust, 19, 98, 119, 121, 125

O

overcome, 121–22

P

perversion, 120, 123

prayer, 6, 64, 68, 94, 124, 142, 144–45

presence, 30, 50, 63, 74, 109, 123–24, 126–27, 141–42

prophets, 8, 76, 106

protector, 106–7

R

rejection, 73, 95–97, 99, 112–13

S

self-rejection, 99, 112

sins, 81, 131

sleep, 49, 62, 118–19

suddenly, 30, 35

U

undetectable, 138

V

victim, 103, 106

voice, 95

W

witchcraft, 28–29, 129

www.ingramcontent.com/pod-product-compliance
Lightning Source LLC
Chambersburg PA
CBHW030116100526
44591CB00009B/412